ENDA W

The Small Things

AND OTHER PLAYS

ENDA WALSH

The Small Things

AND OTHER PLAYS

The Ginger Ale Boy
Disco Pigs
misterman
bedbound
How These Desperate Men Talk
The Small Things
Lynndie's Gotta Gun
Chatroom

with a Foreword by the author

THEATRE COMMUNICATIONS GROUP
NEW YORK

The Small Things and Other Plays is published
by Theatre Communications Group, Inc., 520 Eighth Avenue,
24th Floor, New York, NY 10018-4156,
by special arrangement with Nick Hern Books Limited.

This volume was first published in Great Britain by Nick Hern Books Limited.

A CIP catalogue record for this book is available from the Library of Congress.

ISBN 978-1-55936-403-4

Cover image by Sarah Weal
Cover design: Ned Hoste, 2H
First TCG edition, November 2011

Contents

Foreword

I was a complete and utter waster in my twenties. There was probably something for me in Dublin in the early 1990s. But I didn't see it.

I moved to Cork then and I fell in with a bloke called Pat Kiernan who had started Corcadorca Theatre Company. There was twelve of us working with Corcadorca within two months. We were paid by the social welfare. It kept us off the streets and in a little theatre called the Triskel Arts Centre in Cork City. It was a time of stout and crisps and I think we genuinely all liked each other (for a while). Pat Kiernan was the real talent though. He actually read plays! He was also an excellent director and we rode on his energy and spark devising work sporadically over a year or so and playing it on the small stage of the Triskel to a developing and devoted fan base. I was working in theatre. I was directionless. But I was with friends. And we were directionless together.

During this time I had become the designated writer. I don't really know why. I probably had notions about myself and I suppose I wanted to become a foil to Pat's natural talent for direction. I had an idea of a play about a ventriloquist who has a nervous breakdown. A musical comedy! Pat encouraged me to write it… but I had to keep everyone in the group happy… so the play's shape and characters were decided on what we had in the room. It had songs in it because the guy who wrote music had to be kept busy and out of the pub. It had dance routines because there was a couple of restless dancers wanting to choreograph something/ anything. Everyone wanted a monologue. Fair enough. It was pretty makeshift stuff. I had no idea what I was doing. *The Ginger Ale Boy*'s a mess but it has some ability in there, I suppose. The production was fantastic though and that was all Pat. Leaving that play behind, I knew I had to write a proper play for Pat and something cheap also. We were broke. The stout and crisps continued. Thank Christ. I'd write a two-hander.

I had seen a young actress Eileen Walsh in a play by Gina
Moxley called *Danti Dan*. She was completely unique. So I
decided to write her a play. *Disco Pigs* is a jumble of things. A
failed relationship I had with a twin, my relationship with the
Cork dialect as a Dublin man, the explosive nightlife of the city
at that time and our company's participation in that nightlife.
The play wrote itself in two weeks, was hugely naive but had a
language that surprised me and somehow captured something
about the city. We were blessed with finding Cillian Murphy
who was still in college doing Law. Himself and Eileen clicked
and were extraordinary together. And again it was Pat Kiernan
who captured the pulse and energy of where we were in our
lives at that particular time in his superb production. For two
years we were opening festivals all over the world. The stout
was put on hold as we socialised on more classier beverages.

As a reaction to the urban cool of *Disco Pigs* I found myself
writing a nasty rural thriller called *misterman*. That play went
on to influence later plays. It's very thin on the page but the life
and lies of the central character Thomas felt very large and dark
on stage. I ended up playing Thomas. It's a one-man show. It
was a dangerous thing to do as I'm not a natural actor but I
loved the wildness of carrying a show alone and the sense of it
all about to fall apart at any moment. I understood only then the
power needed to be on stage and that a strong character will
demand a certain logic for a play, a particular structure for the
play. It was something I suppose I inherently knew but the
experience of being on stage with my own text spelled the
lesson out to me. As much as the writer is always 'on', I needed
to find ways of disappearing and allowing character to just be. A
consequence of acting in *misterman* was that I inevitably fell
out badly with my co-creator Pat Kiernan. This was devastating.
Corcadorca went on to building huge shows and I went the
other direction. I needed to make smaller-scale work and try to
get myself talking to myself in a stronger, more personal way.

bedbound was my first effort away from Pat and towards
myself. It's essentially about the relationship between me and
my dad. It's wild but also very honest. A love letter to my sick
dad at the time. Both characters are tortured monsters and it
takes a significant journey for the audience to arrive at some

empathy for these creatures. The play struck a chord. This was pleasing. It's a hard piece and the redemption of the ending doesn't always sit for people... but it ended the way it should have and I was glad to be a part of it.

Disco Pigs, misterman and *bedbound* were translated into many languages and over this three- to four-year period I was making connections with European theatremakers. I've always been embarrassed by my own voice and my characters tend to be battered and trapped by language. The actual words in the plays were meaning less to me and directing *bedbound* in German and Italian, and seeing my work in various languages, started giving me a clearer sense of form and structure. The shorter plays in this volume were written for European colleagues and seem like exercises in form and atmosphere more than anything else.

The Small Things was a play written about the relationship of my dead father with my still alive mother. It's a tightly spun machine of a play that searches out silences. It has this ceaseless rhythm to it which I must have been conscious about when writing. It feels like it was written in one sitting. Of mine it's still my favourite. Obviously I love the characters a lot and the ending I really needed, but the world of it and what these characters are experiencing is still a mystery to me.

The final play in this volume is *Chatroom*. A play I loved writing. A play unlike anything I have written. It doesn't even feel like mine. But I think I wrote it from a perspective within me. My fifteen-year-old self. I'm immensely proud that so many kids have performed it all over the world now and it speaks to them somehow.

I've always tried to get out of the way when writing these plays. Writing a foreword seems somewhat disingenuous then. But here they are, these early plays, and all together. Thanks for taking the time and I hope in reading them they throw something at you.

Enda Walsh, 2010

THE GINGER ALE BOY

The Ginger Ale Boy was first performed by Corcadorca Theatre Company at the Granary Theatre, Cork, on 30 March 1995 (previews from 27 March). The cast was as follows:

BOBBY	Eanna Breathnach
BARNEY	Bríd Ní Chionola
MOTHER	Fiona Peek
DANNY	Myles Horgan
LOVE INTEREST	Sorcha Carroll
TELEVISION WOMAN	Valerie Coyne
ICE-CREAM MAN / CHORUS	Dominic Moore
MAUREEN / CHORUS	Anita Cahill
COMMUNITY / CHORUS	Christine Utzeri
COMMUNITY / CHORUS	Michael McCabe

Director	Pat Kiernan
Designers	Pat Kiernan and Harry Moore
Lighting Designer	Paul Denby
Music	Eoghan Horgan
Costume Designer	Joy McAllen

Characters

BOBBY

BARNEY

MOTHER

DANNY

LOVE INTEREST

TELEVISION WOMAN

ICE-CREAM MAN

MAUREEN

DOG ONE

DOG TWO

Also chorus, dancers, members of the community

The set is dominated by two large staircases that sweep up dramatically into a small boy's box bedroom. Up in that room a boy/man is sleeping. This is BOBBY. *The alarm sounds loudly and he is up fast and suddenly holding a ventriloquist dummy,* BARNEY, *on his knee.*

Music begins and BOBBY's *manager* DANNY *appears, singing, as* DANCERS *dance.*

DANNY. He walked... cross the river towards Rio.
　　　He talked... to many natives on the way.
　　　He asked... 'Is it found here in Brasilia?'
　　　They said... 'Fame is a stranger here.'

In the bedroom BOBBY *and* BARNEY *run through their ventriloquist routine.*

　　　So he ran... 'cross the deserts of Kurdistan.
　　　He rang... on every bell in Istanbul
　　　He asked... five thousand belly dancers.
　　　They said... 'Fame is a stranger here.'

　　　Oh Fame, my rosary.
　　　Fame, my PhD.
　　　Everyone's lookin' for the high life.
　　　You gotta get ya through
　　　Life's like a funeral parlour.
　　　With Fame that body ain't you.

　　　Back home... so tired and yes, bewildered.
　　　The boy... told his mother he tried but failed.
　　　She said... 'Just settle down, my sweet little one,' (*Sigh.*)
　　　And she told him... this story of a family.

BOBBY *drops* BARNEY *and dresses himself.*

　　　Through hardship and sickness this family battled.
　　　Through thick and through thin they fought.

And just when their hearts grew weaker.
Fame saw the youngest and thought:
'I'll give him… a gift that folks would die for.
I'll make him… a tap-dancing superstar.'
'Cause Fame… no matter how you sweat your tail off.
It's Fame… that does the searching near and far.

BARNEY *gets to his feet, runs down the stairs and performs an outrageous tap-dance routine.*

Oh Fame… elusive morning.
Oh Fame… rosary.
Oh Fame… I'm gettin' closer.
Fame… just you wait and see!

The song ends and DANNY *and the* DANCERS *are gone.*

A clock is heard ticking.

BOBBY'*s* MOTHER *cleans a toilet. She's from Liverpool.*

MOTHER. Did you leave that mess in the toilet?! It's like bloody Pearl Harbour in there! Can't you learn how to piss straight?! At least crouch down and give an aim a little! I'll tell you, sweetheart, one look at that rim, too late mind you, and I thought, 'Father's son! Oh, here we go! What's this?' I'm out with the scouring powder… knees on soiled toilet rug… giving the loo floor the once-over with your father's old knickers. I catch my reflection in the silver flusher handle and I mouth my epitaph… 'There must be more to life than this!' Arm down, I finally dislodge that enormous creature from the toilet bowl. Felt like one of those great English dam-busters from the great colonial days. All the time I'm gripping the edge of the toilet bowl with sheer peril, when… 'Oh fuck me sideways!' Little yellow puddles of piss hang about the rim like yesterday's Smarties down in our local pool. 'Oh Bobby!'

BOBBY (*aside*). My mother.

MOTHER. And it's not that I haven't tried! I have tried! I have! I was there! Twenty-five hours a day if necessary! A slave! A little baby cough is all it took and there I'd be, pounding that

baby-sized cough right out of those baby-sized tiny lungs!
'Stop hitting the baby!' your father would say! 'I'm saving
the poor dear's life!!' What did he ever know? What does he
know now? What do men know about babies, anyway? But
you, son! I gave you, I did! I gave you the best... I gave you
them, Bobby! I gave you the best years... the best years of
your father's life! The least you can do is talk to the
miserable old bastard!

BOBBY. Hello, Dad.

MOTHER. Don't you 'Hello, Dad' him!! 'Thank you, Dad!
Thank you, Dad!' Education doesn't come cheap and he
should know! Do you think he liked crawling out of bed at
5.30... a.m. 'A' bloody 'M', and just to stop and started
another in the p.m. A bit of respect is all that's asked,
Bobby!! Break his heart! Crawling home all knackered for a
two-hour sleep just to start it all over again! He was never
there for me either! Is it any wonder he's the way he is?!
Appreciation, Bobby! Be glad of that full-colour poster with
English football memorabilia!

BOBBY. I never wanted that stuff! We're Irish!

MOTHER. Not me! I'm English, bread and bloody buttered and
given half the chance, boy, I'd get out of this Emerald Pile!
But like you, son, I'm stuck... and worse still, we're stuck
where we are! My motto's 'Make the Most'. When your days
and nights send forth only misery and shite, think daisies and
blossom smells! It pays to keep the lid off your dreams,
Bobby! How do you think I've stuck with your father for so
long?

BOBBY *comes down the stairs having dressed in a black
velvet 'showbiz suit'.*

BOBBY. The business of the day is me. These days, it always
is. I'm ready, it seems. Bourbon cream in hand, she clears a
space, and I stand there ready.

BARNEY *hops off the floor and sits on* BOBBY*'s knee.*

MOTHER. Barney looks good. So what do you have for me?

BOBBY. Then I begin. It's me and Barney. We're mixing new material with the old. I'm cutting a word too long and adding that one word too less. The words are flashing in front of my eyes... I grab them and I speak them out. From him or me. I speak words now, though you can't tell, can you? My lip-control is flawless. My tongue connects with my hand and it becomes Barney's tongue. His head pivots on my hand. To me, Barney's become alive. With lever and rope, yes, but most of all... it's me... I'm the one who's woken him. Without me he's nothing. A twist of my hand is all it takes and a pinch of the lever, and with that look, Barney's always there for me. 'Aren't you, Barney? You'll always be by my side.' And inside I'm listening to my rhythm. Our rhythm. The rhythm of words. Funny words. I deliver that line and receive those applause and I grab at a word again... seamlessly. Like when I did my balloon-folding act... But this is what we've trained for. This here. Just me and Barney. And I watch my mother laugh. Like a cloud, her fat changes shape with each chuckle. A blast of laughter lifts the kitchen table, and somewhere in the room... a jam jar rattles. She's looking and laughing at Barney, but it's me that she loves.

MOTHER. I like it! Oh, it's... it's... it's very funny!

BOBBY. Really?

MOTHER. Yes! Not as good as your granddad, mind you! But you're good, Bobby! Best in Cork City, I'd say. Very good! Here, have a biccie!

BOBBY. Thanks.

MOTHER. They're the ones you like! Who needs diets, hey?! They're only an excuse for more packaging! Try one of those iced shorties.

BOBBY. I will.

MOTHER. It's what's inside that matters. That's right, isn't it, Bobby?!

BOBBY. No one could ever find your inside.

A pause as they do nothing. Then:

MOTHER. Are you going to try and get outside today?

A pause.

BOBBY. Yes, I'll try.

MOTHER. You'll try and go outside?

BOBBY. I said I would!

MOTHER. Make the most!!

BOBBY. She carries on like that until she gets her fifth cup of Nescafé down her. I'm not my own any more… but I can wait. We'll sit in the kitchen until Danny comes over.

They wait in silence for a long period.

Jazz music. DANNY *enters with full Cork swagger.*

DANNY. Casual in the daytime – Shirt and tie in the evenings. A summer's morning and Christ I'm hot… but just the right side of hot, mind you. I make casual and skip outta my beat-up Mazda… when just then!… A twenty-something leggy blonde purrs by and gives me a 'want me' smile. I want her back and growl out my stake for those juicy hips. (*Growls while combing back his hair.*) I break into a short-lived trot that finds me hand-on-gate entering the garden from hell. A ferocious puny mongrel foams and displays for me his deadly fangs in monstrous, man-eating barks! Diligently I strike out and kick the little doggy, sending him five yards careering towards a tangled rosebush of dirty coal sacks. Like a good-lookin' lanky Cork City striker I clench my goal and take your 'Olés'! I'll tell ya, boy, I'll leave ye stiff and callin' out for more! A medium close-up catches my satisfaction… (*Freezes into a smile. Stops.*) And takes me down this garden path of jungle weeds and up-turned turds. My crushed tanned slip-on finds one of these poos but I walk on regardless yet puffing. A thick-piled carpet waits inside. I'll make my deposit there.

Music stops.

MOTHER. Danny!! Come in, love! Nice to see ya!

DANNY. Nice carpet! Very nice! (*Wipes his shitty shoe on the carpet.*)

MOTHER. Why, thank you! (*Smells the air.*) Nice aftershave!

DANNY (*smells the air*). Yes. Very nice. Indeed. (*Turns to BOBBY.*) Hey, my little man!

DANNY *fires an imaginary pistol at* BOBBY *while making that noise.*

BOBBY. My agent. He lyrically waltzes my mother about the sitting room, making idle remarks about the decor as if he were in the Copa Cabana.

DANNY. Oh, that's nice! Oh, I like that, yes! Oh, it has a certain…

MOTHER. Niceness?

DANNY. Exactly! Plus more. Character plus style. Art-déco plus home-naturale.

MOTHER. Bobby says it's old-fashioned.

DANNY. Sure old-fashioned is new!

MOTHER. Really?

DANNY. Peruse at your pleasure the meteoric resurrection of the maxi-skirt.

MOTHER. I will! Have you got one to spare?

DANNY. Not yet no.

BOBBY. A bisexual transvestite like Danny makes her feel twenty years younger… despite Danny matching her for years… if not older. It's hard to tell with Danny. Mother says that he might have his faults but give him a tub of foundation and a little pad and he's a wizard. Mind you, his legs are knackered.

DANNY. I've killed a fortune in popsocks over the years! The pains you put yourself through to give others pleasure. You know, Danny La Rue cried himself to sleep every night for forty-five years!

MOTHER. Did he?

DANNY. He did.

BOBBY. They both stay on showbiz-speak and move me centre-stage again.

MOTHER. I can feel it in my waters, Danny, he's ready.

DANNY. But can he…

MOTHER. Danny, I laughed, love! I did!

DANNY. Oh, he's a good boy, all right!

MOTHER. Well, I've watched him, haven't I? Watched him well.

DANNY. I just need the nod, girl, that's all.

MOTHER. I'm nodding, Danny.

DANNY. Can he be trusted?

A pause. BOBBY *shifts in his seat and* BARNEY *turns to stare at* DANNY.

I won't let it happen again.

A pause.

MOTHER. It's a different show from last year's. He's got Barney, hasn't he?

BOBBY. I stop listening and leave, leaving them with me in the kitchen. I pass by my father's butterfly collection, framed up in the hallway. They're all the same kind. All a yellow colour. I like them. I think about my dad. How he hasn't spoken for about two years, and I think… that's not too sad, really. There are worse things than staying quiet in life. I think so, anyway.

A pause. BOBBY *closes his eyes*.

BOBBY. I can tell that she's coming over again. It's that feeling I have... and just like before.

LOVE INTEREST *appears and* BOBBY *opens his eyes*.

And when I look up, it is her, my old doll. A garden with holocaust in its eyes peeps up and starts to bloom. Stretched dog turds wipe away, leaving only lavender and lemon smells. The rust on the gate turns good as she pirouettes down our garden path... paved in quartz. Our mongrel dog rolls onto his back and starts cooing. She rubs his stomach and him, like some tiny baby, seems to smile... and doesn't even try to get up on her leg the way he does to others. Now she's by me. It's Fame. She whispers something... but it's lost... I strain to hear the next. She then takes my hand in hers and we watch the dog, who's made up like he's off to Crufts. She whispers something... I strain to hear, and grab her next word. And she faces me, hand in hand once more, whispering. 'I can't hear what you're saying. What is it you're saying, love?' (*Pause*.) I must get ready. (*Pause*.) And it looks and smells of summer outside here. For the first time in so long... it feels like summer.

An ICE-CREAM MAN *and his wife* MAUREEN *appear*.

ICE-CREAM MAN. Maureen!! Maureen!! Keep that engine running, girl!! Ohhhh, Jayney Mackers!! I'm seein' hate in your eyes now, boys!! Besieged I am by screaming fusiliers while my little tin trench shudders 'neath your tiny hands!! Sure, is it any wonder your mammies toss ye outways! Not one 'please' to pass your lips, I'll launch my war cry!! 'Wait your fucking turn, boyo!!' A musketeer of the ice-cream world! A Richard Clayderman of the vanilla whip, I assume the aggressive and cones in fist, I'll whip up my attack. Now, let's have ya!! Just look at the form on those cones. Now be honest with me, sunshine, and tell me cert, have ya ever seen the cream so solid? WALLOP!! I deliver it swift and gather the readies! But head up and eyes follow, to spy your full platoon salivatin' and yieldin'

bullets of want my ways! And one by one I power my
pillars of cream deep inside your groping guts! But still
more and more. 'Maureen!!' Strengthening my stronghold I
place Maureen on crisps and sweeties. 'Well, get to it, love!
It's now I need ya more than ever!' FIRE!!! A volley of
plain whips lightly coated in a choccy shell slams your
front line. Quickly I gather and silenced, nay, petrified, ye
limp away, lickin' your wounds. But Christ and double
Christ! Your second division in a fiery quickstep
manoeuvre in on all sides. As reliable as a Wet Tuesday,
Maureen stands firm... rocketing out a round of cheese and
onion! 'Oh, nice firing, Maureen! Splendid use of the
plastic bag! Dynamite, girl!!' But what's this? Good Lord,
no! Ohh nooo! Here he comes. 'Cover me now, Maureen!'
Here's a man with real armature! 'I'm going in for the
Chocolate Sundae Surprise... "Surprise" being it will cost
him a Sister McAuley.' (*Prays*.) Christ watch over your one
and only in his hour of greed! WALLOP AND WHIP!!
Ohh, yes!! Yes!! Yes!! Yes!! Alone I'll take ye all on!! 'My
ice-cream wizardry will for ever leave ye nobbled! For,
cone in hand, I'll never be toppled!' NEVER!!!
'Maureen!!! My work is done here! Drive on, girl!'

'Teddy Bears' Picnic' is heard. He calms down. MAUREEN
remains silent beside him.

Beautiful, hah? Sure, that's beautiful music! And look how
our battlefield becomes a playground. Good Christ, that's
great news, that is. While only earlier did ye sneer in hateful
jibes, sure now you're all smiley and ice-pop-like. 'Bye-bye
Mr Ice-Cream Man!' I hear ye say. 'Well, bye-bye buachailli
agus cailini!' And I watch as ye run by my van, waving and
laughing. I toss ye some penny chews. 'Don't forget to brush
your teeth, now! 'Cos with good comes bad.' And you all
love me 'cos I bring the sun and I'm the ice-cream man.
What was pain for me brought happiness to you, isn't that it,
hah? Sure, that's life! Hey, Maureen? (*Pause*.) She doesn't
answer me... Just drives on to the next place. (*Pause*.) We're
fighters, my girl and me... and we do fight. I bark most, I

suppose, but it's my bite that we feed on. It's my bite that keeps us in close. Time has scoffed her face and flattened her chest and fattened that heart but Maureen just sighs and says, 'Where there's hope, there's life! Where there's hope, there's life. Where there's hope, there's life.' And d'you know, a day doesn't go by when I'm adding on to that hope. I'm adding hope to hope. And what hopes have I got without the fight? What life have I when nothing's beneath? Nothing. (*Pause*.) To become like this place.

'Teddy Bears' Picnic' stops.

Sun doesn't shine like true summer here. Here the sun scorches. On these streets, wild dogs, like pinballs, they fire out of houses reeking of shit and boarded up in cellophane. The houses, they lean like headstones. And there's no children. And there's no sounds. (*Long pause*.) And there's nobody here. Just these hungry dogs. The people they live inside… afraid to leave for the outside they say. It's poverty on these streets. (*Sniffs the air.*) It smells of poverty to me. (*Long pause*.) 'We're not needed here, Maureen.' The fight's too big.

BOBBY. I'd like a plain cone, please.

ICE-CREAM MAN. Please.

A pause.

BOBBY. I did say please. Please.

ICE-CREAM MAN. Aren't ya hot inside that thing? Ya must have an awful sweat on ya!

BOBBY. I don't think so. Not really.

ICE-CREAM MAN. A T-shirt.

BOBBY. No.

ICE-CREAM MAN. A T-shirt's the thing! Never too old to wear one, either. And sure look at ya! You're young. Twenty-one, maybe?

BOBBY. Twenty-five actually.

ICE-CREAM MAN. Knock-a-dee knock and key of the door!

BOBBY. That's right.

ICE-CREAM MAN. And open wide! (*Hands* BOBBY *his ice cream.*)

BOBBY. Thank you!

> *The* ICE-CREAM MAN *suddenly grabs* BOBBY*'s hand. He stares, examining* BOBBY*'s face.*

ICE-CREAM MAN. I know you. I remember you. I remember your face.

> BOBBY *pulls back his arm.*

You're that fella! Bobby!!! (*Laughs.*)

> *A single violin begins to play a fast, rhythmic tune.*

> *The* ICE-CREAM MAN *is heard shouting in the darkness.*

BOBBY. I'm trying to leave and still hearing that loud, fat hulk warbling out my song! For all the world to hear the Cock-eyed Optimist is out and about as that bastard man rounds up the troops like I'm the Sunday roast on everybody's lips.

ICE-CREAM MAN (*roaring*). Bobby!!

BOBBY. And what now?! What do they want? More? To them, I'm still 'him'. A silver-sequinned dreamer who's got a new line on hope!! Oh, why did I leave?? Inside it's safe! I want for the inside right now!!

ICE-CREAM MAN. Bobby!!!

BOBBY. Oh, fuck it!!! I wanted a summer but now look!! Trembling like some baa-baa lamb, this is my place too!!

ICE-CREAM MAN. Bobby!!

> *Violin stops. The sound of* DOGS *viciously barking.*

DOG ONE. Come to me, you little fucker!

DOG ONE *lunges at* BOBBY, *who jumps away.*

BOBBY. No dog will eat me! Least of all a bony fart like you!!

BOBBY *kicks the dog away.*

DOG TWO *lunges towards* BOBBY.

Another! And this time more alive and up to my fight!

DOG TWO. Who allowed you out, boy?

BOBBY. I'm ready for you, you mass of fleas!

DOG TWO. I'll rip you to pieces!

BOBBY. Then take me on! I'll eat you up and shit ya out!

DOG TWO *lunges at* BOBBY.

(*Screams.*) Ahhhhh! (*Pause.*) Open wide, you rabid Bonzo!! (*Kicks out.*)

DOG TWO *is kicked back.*

It's me who's winning this war of nerves! (*Kicks out and strikes.*) Not you! It's feeling like summer again, when there's someone beneath! And it's not me! Bobby's better! Bobby's better! Bobby's better!!

Slow fade out to black.

MOTHER *and* BOBBY *are standing at the kitchen table.* MOTHER *stands silently, watching* BOBBY *pensively stare into nothing.*

MOTHER. Don't just sit there saying nothing! How do you feel?

BOBBY. What?

MOTHER. What do you think?

BOBBY. Fine.

MOTHER. Is that a feeling or a thinking?

BOBBY. I feel fine.

MOTHER. Really?

BOBBY. I think I do. It's great.

MOTHER. 'Great'? Ireland's record in the Eurovision, that's 'great', Bobby! I mean, it's frightening but it's still 'great'... but a television-audition-thingy is 'magnificent'!

BOBBY. It's an interview, Mother.

MOTHER. An informal pizza, a splash of some French wine, two men of the entertainment world tripping over the niceties of stardom. All that's TV parlance for 'he wants you'.

BOBBY. It mightn't mean a thing!

MOTHER. You just have to make the right impression, Danny says.

BOBBY (*snaps*). I know what I have to do!!

MOTHER. All right all right!! Tsch! I've ironed your other shirt, you just need some clean smalls.

A pause.

BOBBY. I'm sorry. I don't feel too well.

MOTHER. I love you, son. You're what's called 'brand new'. When all about is showing up dull and dirty, you're the one carrying the clean flag.

A pause.

BOBBY. I went out today.

MOTHER. Yes, I saw.

BOBBY. It's not all loveliness with me, you know. They haven't forgotten me.

MOTHER. How would you fancy a corned-beef sandwich to tide you over before tonight?

BOBBY *moves up the stairs.*

BOBBY. I took my corned-beef sandwich into Dad and the
television. Four o'clock on the hottest day of the year and
there he sat mouthing Karl Malden's lines on *The Streets of
San Francisco*. He'll watch anything, my dad. One day I
caught his sad eyes glued to this Czechoslovakian cartoon
about a spot that fell in love with a squiggle. And he was
crying. Maybe it was too close to home. Maybe that was it.
(*Pause.*) I left Dad on *The Streets of San Francisco* and came
up here to my room to smarten myself up for this television
man. (*Pause.*) And I'm upstairs now. So this is my life
you're in apparently. It's all too simple when I think of it.
There's me and Barney, Mother and Danny and my girl. And
all of us just trying to keep our heads above to catch that
bright canary yellow. (*Pause.*) I'm ready, I'm told.

BOBBY *goes up, undresses and gets into bed.*

Music. A string quartet plays rhythmless tune.

TELEVISION WOMAN. 'No thanks' – to the lift home! 'No
thanks' – to the toilet roll. No apologies! No goodbyes! Just
leave! My headed notepaper floating on a layer of anchovy
and Bobby swooning goggly-eyed and bloated – a half-
digested pizza spilling out of his gob, doing a Torvill and
Dean down his chin onto his jeans! It was when we both sat
down, menus in hand, Piat d'Or in the other, idle chat about
the waitress… about the decor…

An audio recording of BOBBY *and the* TELEVISION
WOMAN *is heard as* BOBBY*'s face is seen on a television
screen.* BARNEY *plays* BOBBY*'s disastrous evening in the
centre of the stage.*

BOBBY (*recording*). Laura Ashley?

TELEVISION WOMAN (*recording*). Of course!

BOBBY (*recording*). It's nice!

TELEVISION WOMAN (*recording*). What?

BOBBY (*recording*). In moderation!

TELEVISION WOMAN (*recording*). Do you think?

BOBBY (*recording*). Well, I think so.

TELEVISION WOMAN (*recording*). Whereabouts then?

BOBBY (*recording*). A bathroom?

TELEVISION WOMAN (*recording*). What?!

BOBBY (*recording*). A child's room?

TELEVISION WOMAN (*recording*). What about your room, then?

BOBBY (*recording*). What about my room?

TELEVISION WOMAN (*recording*). More wine?

BOBBY (*recording*). Please!

TELEVISION WOMAN. His very best suit a sea of anchovy now! Down Grand Parade like a tinselled chilli… a galloping gourmet that's just been gourmeted! He's jelly. He's all jelly. Never have I seen such an amount of jelly on one person! Excluding your Aunt Vera when she had those thighs on Sandymount Strand! How we'd dread all those summer trips. More cellulite than the combined population of China – I hated that fucking woman!!

BOBBY (*recording*). Butlins?

TELEVISION WOMAN (*recording*). Yes, well, Danny told me.

BOBBY (*recording*). Well, he never told me.

TELEVISION WOMAN (*recording*). What made you cancel?

BOBBY (*recording*). I don't know!

TELEVISION WOMAN (*recording*). Can't you remember?

BOBBY (*recording*). I can't remember!

TELEVISION WOMAN (*recording*). Balloon-folding?!

BOBBY (*recording*). That's right!

TELEVISION WOMAN (*recording*). Exactly what?

BOBBY (*recording*). Endangered species.

TELEVISION WOMAN (*recording*). A favourite?!

BOBBY (*recording*). Armadillo!

TELEVISION WOMAN (*recording*). More wine?

BOBBY (*recording*). Why not!?

TELEVISION WOMAN. His bladder's working overtime, so Lucey Park's a welcome pit-stop. But not welcome enough. He starts moaning…

BOBBY *moans himself.*

Walking on in an audible drone. But it's free-form walking that he walks! Each step an all-new and different style than the last step! Keep this up, I'll give you your own game show on a Thursday. Silly bastard!!

BOBBY (*recording*). What are these?

TELEVISION WOMAN (*recording*). Anchovy!

BOBBY (*recording*). Fish?

TELEVISION WOMAN (*recording*). Yes!

BOBBY (*recording*). Baby fish?

TELEVISION WOMAN (*recording*). Adults!

BOBBY (*recording*). Dwarf fish?

TELEVISION WOMAN (*recording*). That's right!

BOBBY (*recording*). Oh my Gawd!

TELEVISION WOMAN (*recording*). What is it?

BOBBY (*recording*). They're staring at me!

TELEVISION WOMAN (*recording*). Have you eaten many?

BOBBY (*recording*). A couple of families!

TELEVISION WOMAN (*recording*). More wine?

BOBBY (*recording*). Of course more wine!

TELEVISION WOMAN. Down Oliver Plunkett Street and he catches his look in a shop window. Like the missing link that Darwin overlooked, he tries to muster a smile... anything... just a little something... but only manages a cross-eyed look and the beginnings of a drool. He's leaking out all over now and as if to prove his point he breaks wind and shits himself.

BOBBY. Oh, Jesus Christ!

TELEVISION WOMAN. Like a bad busker who's missed the ball, he's outside the Post Office singing 'Layla'. He doesn't know the words, just the tune and the dance so he sings them instead. He's singing so loud that a long-limbed girl with a voice like an abattoir asks can she do harmony. 'Harmonise with this!' and like a nasty prop forward, he hands her off onto some toothless fuck. Never have you heard screaming so loud... and she wasn't even in key!

BOBBY (*recording*). I'm not too well!

TELEVISION WOMAN (*recording*). I'll see you Tuesday, then!

BOBBY (*recording*). I've had too much!

TELEVISION WOMAN (*recording*). You'll be fine!

BOBBY (*recording*). I can't perform there!

TELEVISION WOMAN (*recording*). You're a good boy, Bobby!

BOBBY (*recording*). Not in front of them, I can't! I can't go back there!!

TELEVISION WOMAN (*recording*). You're making a scene!

BOBBY*'s face disappears off the television screen.*
BARNEY *makes a fast exit to be replaced by* BOBBY.

TELEVISION WOMAN. Eight thirty on a bright summer's evening, and he's running down Patrick's Street, screaming. Soaked, numbed and stained his teeth have started to wave… and like a blind evangelist, he's got his number eight in sight!

BOBBY. Oh no!

TELEVISION WOMAN. He elbows his way down the bus queue, sending OAPs crashing against the Eason's window. 'Out of my way!!' And reaching into his pocket, and one foot on, and fumbling out his pence, and chucking them at a short, stocky driver, stuck in FM-radio. HE'S ON!!

The COMMUNITY *appear.*

COMMUNITY (*lines divided*). Tell us the one about the fat man!

About the saucepan!

Tell me that one!

Or, what about the back-on!

That bacon one!

Go on!

Do the funny talk!

That swanky one!

Something saucy!

Something for the girls!

I'd say he has!

They all laugh.

Oh, tell us the one about the…

This man walks into a…

Knock, knock!

Paddy who?

D'ya hear the one?

My wife's so…

What d'you call!?

What d'you get?!

This Irish man.

Queer!

Mother-in-law!

I once knew this!

Tell me!!

Go on!!

Give me!!

Come on!

Punchline!

Tell me!!

Go on!!

Give me!!

Come on!

Punchline!!

Tell me!!

Go on!!

Give me!! Come on!

Punchline!!

BOBBY. I don't wait for the bus to stop. I jump! Forgetting about the bus stop I catch the bus stop in the centre of my face!

The COMMUNITY *spit and jeer and whistle.*

Bastards!! I hear angels! Heaven, perhaps? Passing me now, smelling of vinegar chips, designed as football fans striped and moustached. I'm making some joke about their manager being Jesus Christ and how Jesus will always ask for the good high cross. Not being angels, I feel a large-sized hand squeeze a regular-sized chips into my partly conditioned hair. Short of a lemon wedge, I'm now a full-course meal. They're all laughing! Personally I don't see the joke... but then, I can't see a fucking thing... so I close my eyes to. And in there I see me up close... having to get laughs... mouth open first then shut... I'm telling jokes just for you... (*Pause as he's lost for words.*) And I'm running fast then! Things race closer and pass... forward and gone... I'm running through things and them past me. Opening in front... closing behind... pushing me to my bedroom! But still up close my face... my joke face and you by my side! Don't see me like this! So run fast, Bobby! And Bobby's closing closer... closer to my home... my home... that's wet with my tears! I am a funny man! Am I a funny man, Mammy? Am I? (*Pause.*) I'm home. I'm safe.

BOBBY *gets into bed.*

The LOVE INTEREST *appears and mimes a song as another actor sings live.*

LOVE INTEREST. Call me laughable,
    Call me comical,
    Call me ludicrous,
    Call me ridiculous,
    Call me whimsical,
    Call me fanciful,
    Call me preposterous,
    Call me scurrilous...

    But I love him,
    Adore him,
    Respect him
    And trust him,
    Admire him,

Won't tire of him,
Did I say I love him?

Where can I find the words to describe
This wonderful guy of mine?!

She begins to perform a sweet tap dance.

I love him,
Adore him,
Respect him
And trust him,
Admire him,
Won't tire of him,
Did I say I love him?

Where can I find the words to describe
This wonderful,
Adorable,
Beautiful,
Marvellous,
Incredible,
Superlative,
Lovable,
Astonishing,
Completely indescribable, my guy!

The LOVE INTEREST *exits.* BOBBY*'s* MOTHER *appears and during the following she makes her way up the stairs and begins to undress a listless, battered son.*

MOTHER. After Agnes, 'Unlucky' is my middle name. Some people have a monopoly on love, sex or money… mine's 'unlucky'!! (*Sighs deeply.*) Ups-a-daisy, I thread my way out of bed and tear open that plaid green curtain just in time to catch Mr Sun slap on his hat. I spy our idiot neighbours glazed in Baby Oil and Vaseline lying out on their patio like a family of sun-dried tomatoes. Stupid Irish bastards! Me?… I stand half-naked and grizzly… a four-hundred-and-sixty-pound turkey in full sweat… all eyes booking me for their Christmas hamper. Breasts the size of the Pacific, nipples like two

bloated onion rings, I fasten them into a bra that previously
housed a small colony of knackers. I'm a big girl, all right!
But big is best. (*Pause*.) Eclipsing our honeyed love nest, I
sidestep and watch as a heavenly shard of handsome sunlight
picks out my husband Brendan. He farts out his morning
chorus… rolls over revealing to me his manhood… catches
my gawk… sighs and promptly rolls back. Gone are the days
of early-morning passions when little trips to the bathroom
ended in glorious bed-wrestling. He'd half-nelson me into a
kiss and whisper sweet nothings until he got his scrambled
eggs. Nowadays his lips only warm to packet soup and hot
cornflakes. We didn't drift apart, him and me… we started off
on opposite platforms until our Expressways moved out.
(*Pause*.) I pull on my knickers, a dressing gown borrowed off
the Khmer Rouge and stamp into my fluffy canary-yellow
slippers. I'm in a real state but I'm done past caring. I have my
reasons. I used to be the Belle of the Ball, now I just run the
cloakroom. People don't set out to live in a damp hole. Fate
just pins you together. In life, most people end up with the
things they don't really want… it gives those who have it all
something to look down at. That's my service to society. I'm
the breadline without the bread. I mean, just look at this
house! We're the same! Our backs all pebble-dashed in a
blotchy overcoat, our fronts all fenced up in a rusty wiry brim.
We're the joke on everyone's lips. I am the English shit on
their shoes. They say that Irish eyes are smiling. At what?
They say that the Irish are neighbourly and courteous. At what
cost? They make no mention of the bigotry! No mention how
begrudging has finally outshone Ireland's previous favourite
pastime of kicking the living shit out of its children. I'm living
in Europe's coal bunker! A foreigner living on the edge of
civilisation. A land where 'idle gossip' can drown little born
babies. This island's sinking out here and still I can hear my
sweet dad say, 'Oh, Sal! Hey, Ireland! The grass is greener
over there!!' Well, it's not, Dad! It's not green or anything so
picture-book! I was the one who was green when I was waved
onto that boat! They confused hospitality with hostility and
they have to be told the truth! Ireland is a crumbling shithole!

She stares down at BOBBY *sleeping.*

He's my ticket out of here. My hopes rest in him. He's the only thing I have. And he's mine. He's my boy Bobby and I love that boy.

BOBBY. I'm asleep.

MOTHER. Danny's delighted! It's official!

BOBBY. I want to sleep!

MOTHER. Tryers sleep while doers do! Right this minute it's practice that needs doing!

BOBBY. Oh, fuck it!

MOTHER. Ohhhh! Bless you!

She shows him a champagne bottle and glasses.

Champagne!

BOBBY. We can't afford that.

MOTHER. Why not? Why can't we, hey? Why the fuck not? Besides, it's ginger ale, really! Same difference. The magic's in the bubbles. It's a prezzie from Danny!

BOBBY (*down*). Great.

They drink.

MOTHER. Drink enough it's like living your dreams. Your dad's dead proud, Bobby.

BOBBY. Did he say anything, then?

MOTHER. It's a TV performance, not the second coming! He smiled a bit, you know. Anyway, he can watch it himself on the box. There's only ever rubbish at that time, anyway. So how does it feel? Excited? Bobby, you needed that last turn to put things straight, hey?! Your granddad would be dead proud too. Of course, had telly arrived in his day, he'd have his prime-time sliced out and then who knows what magical journey I'd have taken!

BOBBY. She knew about the balloon-folding set.

MOTHER. That's right, Danny told her.

BOBBY. What's this about Butlins?

MOTHER. We had plans, that's all.

BOBBY. Was she told about the rest?

MOTHER. We were selling your name and not the past but what's to come! Everything's behind and you've got it all in front!

BOBBY. What have I left behind?

MOTHER. You've left plenty!

BOBBY. How can you tell me that something's changed when it's me who's waking with the past and not you.

MOTHER. I know things.

BOBBY. How do you know things?

MOTHER. I know things because a mother knows best, because this is me as well as you, because out of me came you, because it's me who's clearing up the mess, because I have a dream, because I was here to pick you up when you were nothing… when they made you nothing, it was me who wrapped you in and keeped you safe because I'm your mother and because I belong to what's been, Bobby!

A pause. She holds him in an embrace.

Bobby, once upon a time not so long ago, there was just me and your dad. Fresh off the boat and into the welcoming arms of my blue-eyed beau… I was chuffed… and spread before me at grabbin' distance was a life of wonderful ambition. Back then big beech trees were our neighbours. Copper-coloured and four times as big as our homely den. And these yellow butterflies that your dad would arrive in with after work and he'd let them fly about the house. It was all so beautiful. Everything was. I'd spend a lot of time looking out on those trees. To me it felt as if Nature herself

were handing out a wad of copper fifties and what with me
being a one-person queue I was sure of a handsome bounty.
And I knew then, Bobby, that Fate was sizing me up. I
needed a baby. I'd look out and watch little kids run about
with fists of frogspawn and mouths of acid drops and I'd
imagine a child of my own being part of a gang or, better
still, right beside his own loving mam. In 1967 on a hot
sticky night I was parcelled up and dropped down to the
Mercy and when you popped out, son, you were all wide-
eyed but quiet as if you were woken from a dream. And I
took my little baby boy back to that copper-coloured light
and those little yellow butterflies but they pulled everything
down and left instead only grey. But when I lay you down
on my bed, Bobby, you lit up the house in a light of your
very own. So we learnt to look out, didn't we? Out at the
others and we planned to turn that grey back to what's right.
Your dad too stuck those butterflies behind that frame…
'And one day I'll let them go! One day when it's colour I
see!' That was our plan, Bobby. Still is with me. (*Pause*.)
Eight years go flashing by and right off the blue comes big
sis Daisy! 'Ireland!' she says, 'Top of the mornin' to ya and
all that lark… but where's the fuckin' donkeys?'

She laughs, as does BOBBY *a bit*.

And then she gave you Granddad's suitcase. Do you
remember that day, Bobby?

BOBBY. Yes.

MOTHER. And when you opened that suitcase, love…
oooooooohhh… to see that face… Just like little baby Jesus,
except real.

BOBBY *takes* BARNEY *out of a box*.

And you didn't grab or tug like kids are supposed to do, your
touch was soft, Bobby. You reached down and picked up
Barney like he himself was a little toddler. And you put him
on your knee and your hand into his back. Do you remember
that, son? You worked him real gentle. How did you know

what to do? 'Christ, Daisy, look at my one and only!!' 'It's like our dad all over except miniature and alive,' she said. And that's what I thought, son… I thought… 'This is it. This is my life.' And that night, and how can any of us forget that night… you sat in the kitchen with Barney on your knee… me, Daisy, the dog and your dad… all eyes and all ears. And then you said, 'What do you have in your ears there, Barney?'

BOBBY. Spinach.

MOTHER. Spinach? Oh my God, that's terrible!

BOBBY. I know. I planted carrots.

MOTHER. And that was it! You started on the road to variety! The whole world watching your hand with me to guide. You are funny, Bobby… and funniness spells power.

BOBBY*'s* MOTHER *kisses his head and takes* BARNEY *away, leaving* BOBBY *alone in his room.*

BOBBY. I'm on tomorrow afternoon… our community centre… in front of all of them. (*Pause.*) I have my own story to tell, too.

BOBBY *lies down on his bed. His* MOTHER *is seen polishing* BARNEY.

MOTHER. Goodnight, Bobby. Don't let the bedbugs bite.

BOBBY. I'll try.

MOTHER. Nighty! Nighty!

BOBBY. Sleepy welly! (*To us.*) Goodnight.

In a light, the LOVE INTEREST *appears.*

LOVE INTEREST. I'm standing outside Cash's clock with more backside than a Land Rover overcharged into my hip-cracking jodhpurs. Winter '92 and it's coming down real hard. Cork is stuck in a grey monsoon and all the weather lady can do is smile an ironic smile, wave across another killing weather front, and banish me to yet another in a long succession of 'bad-hair days'. My luck's out. I deserve better than all of this. Some sorry sight, chewing on a fast-food carton and crying uncontrollably, catches my gaze and gives me the benefit of smelling her up close. Inhaling deeply, I gag, murmur the obligatory 'Pardon me!' and pan her aside with my big black umbrella and just in time too it seems... to catch this thick grey cloud of pigeons swoop down onto Winthrope Street while thankfully scattering the buskers. I see him. He must be my blind date, I think. Head high above the others, outfitted in stiff, horny gel and ham-fisted smiles, he struts a constipated strut, cooing in my direction.

BOBBY *speaks his lines from his bed and still asleep, as* BARNEY *plays him meeting the* LOVE INTEREST.

BOBBY. I'm Bobby.

LOVE INTEREST. I'm your Love Interest.

BOBBY. So how do you like the suit?

LOVE INTEREST. I lie and suddenly find myself under that dangling limb he calls an arm. I'm bundled down Winthrope Street and into The Long Valley like a much-needed keg. 'Jesus, why am I doing this?' Why? Because it's a favour to your sweetheart, Danny... my theatrical agent and sometime playboy... He's got high hopes for this walking kelp-man but Bobby gets nervous so I'm drafted in as a welcome tonic before he goes on tonight, but I'd sooner cuddle up to a cold sore that peck those grimy lips.

BOBBY. Danny calls it 'a balloon-folding act with songs and snippets of comedy'. I've been folding all the usual animals but what with there being a lot of me in the act, I feel sort of compelled to do the odd endangered species while singing some old standards. Gives them an edge, you see! So it is somewhat political, I suppose! I want to be remembered as a variety ecologist, basically! A bit like Sting... but with balloons.

LOVE INTEREST. He's growing hysterical and lets fly with the family album.

BOBBY. Now, that's me with Dad! That's me with Mother! Me and the dog. That's me with Danny. That's me practising with Barney... he's the future! Ohhh, and that's me with my first armadillo. Not bad features, really!

LOVE INTEREST. I might as well be looking at the beer mats... to me he looks the same... Well-stained and coming apart at the edges. Only the armadillo raises a slight flutter, until he promptly blows one up, presenting me with my souvenir.

MOTHER *and* DANNY *enter.*

MOTHER. I see the lovebirds are busy nest-building, Danny!

DANNY (*to* LOVE INTEREST). Hello, love.

LOVE INTEREST (*mocking him*). Hello, love.

MOTHER. So, how's the voice holding up, Bobby? Good and waxed, I hope.

LOVE INTEREST. What does he sing?

MOTHER. 'Cockeyed Optimist'. *South Pacific.*

DANNY. All right! Down the hatch. Tonight's your baptism, Bobby!!

LOVE INTEREST. We're bundled into the back seat like two heavy overcoats while Danny and her giggle in the front... swapping funny anecdotes. He stays quiet, though. All the way to the community centre he stares down, all the time rubbing this piece of fabric in his hand. He's afraid to look out.

She takes his hand in hers.

You'll be fine. You've got nothing to be nervous about. I know what it's like, you know. They're all your neighbours, Bobby.

BARNEY (*as* BOBBY) *has started to cry.*

Bobby?

DANNY. Right!! We've arrived!

MOTHER. I've gone all goose-pimply and butterflies!!

DANNY. This night will go down in balloon-folding folklore!

MOTHER. And we were here!

DANNY. Of course we were!

MOTHER. Front row!

DANNY. Cheering! For you!!

MOTHER. For our boy, Bobby!! Good luck, son!! We'll see ya before the judges have made their decision!

Long pause.

BOBBY (*softly in his sleep*). Help me.

LOVE INTEREST. He still latches onto my hand. Then he looks at me and me at him. (*Pause.*) And it's difficult to say. (*Pause.*) He's petrified. He whispers something… but I can't hear it. He whispers again… but no. (*Pause.*) And he's looking at me mouthing words I can't hear. 'Bobby, I can't hear you. What are you saying to me?'

The opening phrases of music of 'A Cockeyed Optimist' from the musical South Pacific *are heard.* BARNEY *as* BOBBY *stands motionless and petrified, holding a balloon. He attempts to go into his song but cannot do it. His head drops.*

The music suddenly breaks into a big, brash musical number which MOTHER *and* DANNY *perform.*

MOTHER. Whatever happened to…

DANNY. Second best!

MOTHER. Whatever happened to…

DANNY. The incompleted test!

MOTHER. Whatever happened to…

DANNY. Those runners-up!

MOTHER. Whatever happened to…

DANNY. One beneath the top!

MOTHER. Now take if you will
    This guy called…

DANNY. Phil!

MOTHER. Who made it his life to cure dementia.

DANNY. I worked night and day!

MOTHER. Prestige his only pay.
    When honours flooded in he'd say…

DANNY. Don't mention it!

MOTHER. But Phil soon grew,
    To be a fool and incontinent too.
    Yes, Phil he truly failed…

DANNY. And no one would pay my bail!
    They said it's…

MOTHER. Failure!

DANNY. That's what it means!!

MOTHER. Mr Failure!

DANNY. No matter if you eat those greens!

MOTHER *and* DANNY. Failure it seems!
    Pips at your dreams!
    Failure is the rip in your seams!

DANNY. Now let's read on,
    To this case we'll call…

MOTHER. Sharon!

DANNY. Who fancied herself as a belladonna.

MOTHER. I starved and moisturised.

DANNY. De-puffed her puffed-up eyes.
  When bit offers trickled in, she'd say…

MOTHER. Why sure I wanna!

DANNY. Now, Sharon was nothing new.
  She lost her top and her panties too.
  Yes, Sharon nakedly failed…

MOTHER. And no one would pay my bail!
  They said it's…

DANNY. Failure!

MOTHER. That's what it means!

DANNY. Miss Failure!

MOTHER. No matter if you eat those greens!

MOTHER *and* DANNY. Failure it seems!
  Pips at your dreams!
  Failure is the rip in your seams!
  Whatever happened to…? (*Sung eight times as they tap dance.*)

During this, the LOVE INTEREST *is heard…*

LOVE INTEREST. And we're all waiting for 'Cockeyed Optimist'. (*Pause.*) We hear nothing. And we see not even a tear. And a woman nudges me and says, 'Is that all he does?' (*Nods.*) It looks that way on the outside.

MOTHER. It's failure!!

DANNY. Say 'How do you do?'

MOTHER. Here's failure!!

DANNY. Right out of the blue!

MOTHER. Failure's for you and you and you!!

DANNY. Darling, you're nothing new!!

MOTHER *and* DANNY. Boo hoo!!

MOTHER. Failure's got an eye on you!

MOTHER *and* DANNY. Now-owww!!
    Failure is looking at you!!!

Music stops. Alarm-clock noise. BOBBY *rises slowly and stands.*

BOBBY. It's just like back then. (*Pause.*) I woke with the past snapping at my shins, digging at my neck. From bed, to street, to this… to them? I'll pinch myself but nothing's changed. I'll do what I do when things are bad… I'll play at being someone else… adopt a mood. But file me under 'fear' 'cause that's all I've got.

BOBBY *looks around and the* COMMUNITY *are standing looking at him.*

I'm what they want. I'm all they have… they've got nothing but this. It's hate that keeps them simmering and in the chase, my dreams are 'it'! (*Long pause.*) So what if I stop? What if I do like back then and stand my ground? Doing just what they want to see… nothing. Will I feel them eat me up? I close my eyes and remember me just like before. Balloon in hand and whimpering like their lost child. Am I resigned to that ending again? I want for something better but starting out can't start by giving in, could it? (*Pause.*) Or if I take to the spotlight and do my act? Then how far can I run from them? I can't hide inside any more or hide in hope. Perhaps I can hide in love? Let me, please. (*Pause.*) Fear has a knack of clearing up the mess and pointing out what's real and raw but where do I rest my choice? Where? Where do I go? I need telling!! Danny!!

DANNY *appears. He's being filmed by the* TELEVISION WOMAN.

DANNY. Stuck in a medium mid-shot, I recline all Val Doonican-like and like a parish priest with soul I let fly with the comparatives. 'He's a conundrum. A real hybrid, mind you! A social commentator with a conscience that likes to laugh! A student of the giggle! A bibliophile of the gag! Erudite plus wag! A roguish prankster with a laudable soul! Virtuous in intent! Fanciful in content! And a nice boy, too! I'll hear no one say otherwise, either! Kind-like! A paragon of morality, ladies! A chin-up, colours-to-the-mast sort of type!! Unshrinking from that eternal call! Resolute in the game, with the world oyster-shaped and rested in his paw, I've got the knife to prise him free and devour his dream! A season in Butlins will see him true... you'll see!!!'

The LOVE INTEREST *appears in light.*

BOBBY. Why don't you say something?

LOVE INTEREST. What do you mean?

BOBBY. Tell me what to do.

She's suddenly gone.

The talent contest is shown in a ridiculous collage as the COMMUNITY *perform songs, dances, jokes, etc. It ends with the* LOVE INTEREST *singing the song she 'sang' earlier. She sings now with her own voice and is dreadful.*

LOVE INTEREST. I love him,
    Adore him,
    Respect him
    And trust him,
    Admire him,
    Won't tire of him,
    Did I say I love him?

    Where can I find the words to describe
    This completely indescribable, my guy!

She comes 'offstage' and is met by DANNY, *who embraces her and kisses her passionately.*

BOBBY *sees this and is crushed.*

MOTHER *sets up* BARNEY *and a stool.* DANNY *and* MOTHER *put make-up on* BOBBY *during the following.*

MOTHER. Make the most, son! When everything's smeared over in shit and piss, just think daisies and blossom smells!

She hands him a huge bunch of daisies.

Two ninety-nine a bunch! Your dad can do without his burgers and all!! I'll fix us something special for the tea, shall I? Something Englishy in memory of my old dad and your new-found fame! All provided that you're not whisked away on Fortune's Trail! TV chat-show spots, celebrity charades with treble-chinned chaps in double-breasted suits and single-celled wits, you know what I mean!! If so... let me get my shout in now: one-way ticket back to my old Anglia, Bobby, all right! (*Slight pause.*) Anything I can do?

BOBBY (*barely audible*). Yes.

BOBBY looks up to her but his MOTHER is gone. Long pause. BOBBY sits on the stool with BARNEY and the bunch of daisies.

Have all my words come down to this? (*Long pause.*) Where's the song and dance to see us through, hey, Barney? (*Long pause.*) This is it. There's nothing left to say.

BOBBY attempts to work BARNEY but his heart and mind aren't able. BARNEY falls from his hand. BOBBY, sitting and holding a bunch of daisies, allows failure take him.

His MOTHER approaches but can't comfort him. A strong yellow light comes up on them.

Blackout.

The End.

DISCO PIGS

To my parents. A special thank you to Pat Kiernan

Disco Pigs was first performed by Corcadorca Theatre Company at the Triskel Arts Centre, Cork, in September 1996, and subsequently at the 1996 Dublin Theatre Festival.

It received its UK premiere at the Traverse Theatre, Edinburgh, on 7 August 1997, before transferring to the Bush Theatre, London, in September 1997, and then on international tour. The cast was as follows:

| PIG | Cillian Murphy |
| RUNT | Eileen Walsh |

Director	Pat Kiernan
Designer	Aedin Cosgrove
Sound Designer	Cormac O'Connor

Characters

PIG

RUNT

Lights flick on. PIG *(male) and* RUNT *(female). They mimic the sound of an ambulance like a child would, 'bee baa bee baa bee baa!!' They also mimic the sound a pregnant woman in labour makes. They say things like 'is all righ, miss', 'ya doin fine, luv', 'dis da furs is it?', 'is a very fast bee baa, all righ. Have a class a water!' Sound of door slamming. Sound of heartbeats throughout.*

RUNT. Out of the way!! Jesus out of the way!

PIG. Scream da fat nurse wid da gloopy face!

RUNT. Da two mams squealin on da trollies dat go speedin down da ward. Oud da fookin way!

PIG. My mam she own a liddle ting, look, an dis da furs liddle baba! She heave an rip all insie!! Hol on Mam!!

RUNT. My mam she hol in da pain! She noel her pain too well! She been ta hell an bac my mam!

PIG. Day trips an all!

RUNT. Da stupid cow!!

PIG. Holy Jesus help me!!

RUNT. Scream da Pig Mam! Her face like a christmas pud all sweaty an steamy! Da two trollies like a big choo choo it clear all infron! Oudda da fookin way cant jaaaaa!!

PIG. Da two das dey run the fast race speedin behine!

RUNT. Holy Jesus keep her safe. Holy Jesus keep her safe!

PIG. Mamble my dad wid a liddle mammy tear in da eye! I'm da liddle baba cummin oud, Dada, I'm yer liddle baba racer!!!

RUNT. Da trollie dey go on

PIG. an on

RUNT. an on

PIG. an on

RUNT. an on

PIG. an on

RUNT. an on

PIG. an on!

RUNT. My mam she suck in da pain, grobble it up an sweat it oud til da liddle skimpy nighty itgo,

PIG. black wet black.

RUNT. Two gold fishys oudda da bowl!!!

PIG. A gasp gaspin! I'm ja liddle baba commin out! Open up ja big fanny!

RUNT. Trollie stop!

PIG. An leg open!

RUNT. Da fatty nurse schlap on with the rubbery glubs! Stop! An leg open! Da two fat sous pooshhh an poooshh ta spit da babas oud!!

PIG. Push girls push!!

RUNT. Scream da das oudsize!

PIG. Scream da das oudsize!

RUNT. My da he wan fur his din dins real fas, yeah!

PIG. Take your time love!

RUNT. He say, stopwadch in han! Da fannys dey look like donna kebabs!

PIG. Bud looka da liddle baba heads!

RUNT. Pooosh da baba poosh da head!!

PIG. Pooshh Mam poosh!! Poosh da Pig

RUNT. An Poosh da Runt! She wan oud Mama!

PIG. An he wan oud, ta dada!

RUNT. Pooosh sous pooosh!!

PIG. We da liddle born babas!

PIG *and* RUNT. Pooosshhhhhh!

Silence. We then hear the sounds of babies crying. Music.

RUNT. An it wuz.

PIG. Nineteen

RUNT. Seventy-nine.

PIG. An da liddle baby beebas a Pork Sity take da furs bread inta da whirl.

RUNT. Da hop-i-da-hill all Bambi an Thumper!

PIG. Hey looka da liddle bunny, baby!

RUNT. An looka da nursey face, is sall rosey like a buuk full a roses!

PIG. An da two liddle babas all wrappt in pooder, ka nice smell pooder!

RUNT. My mam's nighty pink!

PIG. An my mam's nighty pink!!

RUNT. An my mam she pain no more! Sorta happy wid wat she fart out.

PIG. Bud my mam she cry all blubbery wid Dad sittin on da bed flickin thru da *Echo*!

RUNT. Yeah, Pork Sity was luvly amay bak den.

RUNT. Da peeplah dey really nice. Dey say,

PIG. She's a lovely little thing!

RUNT. Goo ga goo!

PIG. Look the little button nose!

RUNT. Ahhh gaga ga!

PIG. And the fingernails, ahhh look!

RUNT. Goo gee gee!

PIG. She's happy in that pram.

RUNT. Gaa gee goo goo!

PIG. She looks just like her mam.

RUNT. Fuck off ja!

PIG. Nell may bak den an me an she weez take a furs bread inta da whirl. A bobbly baby-boots girl she

RUNT. Runt! An a fat fatty fatso fart by da name a

PIG. Pig! But fatty no more! As ja can say, Slimfast fans!

RUNT. Oud we bounce inta a whirl of grey happiness!

PIG. We wa beautiful amay bak den!

RUNT. *Jar* beautiful! *Jar* beautiful, Pig!

PIG. Beg yer pardon, pal! *Jar* beautiful! Jar beautiful! Da liddle baby babbies a Pork Sity!

RUNT. Sa tell em who was furs sa!

PIG. Runt a cause!

RUNT. Tell em who was secon sa, saucey!

PIG. The Pig!

RUNT. Owney one sec tween da girl an da boy! An us no brudder or sis or anyth!

PIG. Fuckin amaz-zing, man! (*Pause.*) Les go Marbyke, yeah!

RUNT. Righ so!

PIG. Race ya!

PIG *and* RUNT *run racing each other. Sounds of heavy breathing.* RUNT *stops and looks as* PIG *continues.*

RUNT. So off we go! Zoomin as always! Pig's a real fass! Down da Marbyke Bark we go war dem mens an womens do da race an all. I wadch da Pig race an he run really really fass aboud da trak, yeah. Sonia O'Sullivan tinks Pig migh be da superstar star!

PIG. Ya noel ol Sonja… dem lightweight running vests aand panties mean no-ting when ya got the finish line in sites! Ya gotta believe girl… without that yer fuck all! (*To* RUNT.) Les go my place.

RUNT. Me da runnin don matter dat much! But see whadda Pig wear? I choose dem! Splendid! I one step ahead in dat race, race fans! Fashion my life. Was goin down downtown, righ in da bum hole a Pork Sity, sall import ta me, yeah! I noel betta den mos fox down French Crotch Street! Pig, he nee da big big elp, dat fella. Withoud Runt poor Pig look like da sausies withoud da skin. Crap!

PIG. Is a hippyidy happidy birrday for my pal Runt n' me!

RUNT. Happy birrday to you.

PIG. Happy birrday to you, pal too! Seventeen, hah?

RUNT. Seventeen yeah! Pig?

PIG. Yes oh ligh a my life, my liddle choccy dip!

RUNT. Wa colour's love, Pig?

PIG. Love? Don no! Wa sorra love, love?

RUNT. Don no!

PIG. Hoy Mam! Way da din dins! Way da sausies an da saucey, hey Mam! Schlap it there la!!

PIG *and* RUNT *eat. We hear the sounds of them eating mixed with them oinking. They stop.*

RUNT. Las get righly gone, ya on! Cider back a da bed yeah?

PIG. Up up up up up up up up up!

RUNT. Down da gob an grab da lot! Up for it are ya?

PIG. A hippidy happidy in it?

RUNT. Les go!

PIG. Race ya so!

RUNT. Ah fook yes!!

> PIG *and* RUNT *drink. It is a race.* PIG *breaks off and goes to the toilet. Sound of pissing.*

PIG. Good, in't she? Gallon by gallon deep we go! A buddel a rider's an awful ting, yeah, but hey, an wad da fuck! Da ting it works! Inta da skull like ka lawn mower it mix me an Runt all aboud! Two fishys a swillin it back a swillin it back a swillin it back… down da belly an oud da spout! Ders me dad a decoraten per use-jew-al. Give it up will ya! get a job, ja langer!

RUNT. Hey, Pig man!

PIG. Hey luvvy! Dis roam is it all! Da ress a da house is par shitheads an wankers! Dis roam is my kingdom! Pig da king! My bed da trone… da clodes dat Runt did make… sacred! Me an Runt… brudder and sis bud much maw, drama fans! We jar it! We fuckin jar ya know! Excuse me but odders are weak, yeah… like spa children ja drown in da river, I drown my mam an dad *now*! If Dad no so busy wid da wallpaper a cause! Da faggot, scone head!

RUNT. Ta da bum hole shall we go?

PIG. Shall we cause!

RUNT. Quids?

PIG. Pock-full a tens!

RUNT. Regal!

PIG. Les go so!

RUNT. Les go so disco!!

> *Loud disco/techno music follows.* PIG *and* RUNT *scream and chant 'Seventeen'. Music eventually stops. Sound of bus stopping.* PIG *and* RUNT *get on the bus.*

PIG. Las time Pig an Runt eva give mona to da bus… mus a bin a baba, a lease! Why nee ta pass wid any kish? Bus boss he well loaded yeah! Jacussi in sall da bedroams, I bed. So me an Runt jus barrel on!

RUNT. Come here to me!!!!

PIG. Scream da ugly wase fat cunt of a diver!

RUNT. Fook off!

PIG. Say Runt. Problem solve yeah! Easy. He noel his place. Sits. Drive da bus on. Slow. I sees him liddle eyes in da mirror! He scare in da eyes! Pig raise da han... Bus fass now. Good.

RUNT. Bus stop... stop bus!

PIG (*recognises someone*). Oh yes. Yes.

RUNT *laughs*.

Foxy locksy, in it?

RUNT. Is Pig.

PIG (*stands*). A birrday giff! Cova me, girl!

RUNT. Will, Pig.

PIG. Righ so! Hi dee hi!

PIG *mimes kicking Foxy around the place*. RUNT *narrates*.

RUNT. Pig an Foxy go all da way! Pig hate Foxy! One nigh, yeah, Pig he gasp for da glug glug glug glug! Down ta Blackcruel we drool. Off licence war Foxy work. Did work mo like.

PIG. Free drink, pretty please.

RUNT. No ney panic button Foxy he panic. He say I can't Darren. Pig he get da buzz in da ead he wanna fisty!

PIG. I ass ya nice, nice man! Han fuckin ova!

RUNT. You know I can't.

PIG. I fuckin kill ya!

RUNT. Darren!

PIG. I get ja mam fuckin burn her, boy!

RUNT. The boss will kill me, Darr...!

PIG. A shut yer gob, shut yer gob, shut yer gob ya fuckidy-fuck!

PIG mouths RUNT's lines below.

RUNT. Took Pig ten mins smash all buddels in dat drink shap. All but one yeah. Pig take da buddel Bacardi slinky... he kiss da buddel... an off. Pig! Jar pock-full a tens! He stamp na Foxy face. Da nose like tomato itgo squish n' drip drop. Foxy cried, cried like his mam jus bin smack in da ead by da golf club... which she war... nex day.

PIG. Shmackkk!!!

RUNT. Pig hate da Foxy. He hate em.

PIG. Schmack schmack schmack schmack schmack schmack schmack schmack schmack schmack schmack!! An let dat be a less on ya, Foxy! Dis bus is no purr you!!!

Sounds of a quiet bar. Television can be heard. RUNT *and* PIG *look around.* RUNT *whistles 'God Save the Queen'.* PIG *laughs.*

Pig n' Runt stop tear furs. Is a sleepy ol' provo pub ta Pork purr years, yeah! Runt always do dat. Funny ho hey?! (*He laughs.*) No soul drink ere! No one gis a fuck aboud dem nordy bas-turds. Way bodder? News a da week is let dem do each odder in!

RUNT. Use-jew-al?

PIG. Oh yes, darling.

RUNT gets drinks in.

I park a top a da seat by da pool an jus calm an wadch! Good like! Don cost no-ting eeder! I tink bout Foxy an my boot ta jaw face. I let da buzz go bye bye an down my ead it go... Pig breed it oud. Calm brudder calm down. I wadch in real calm now. (*Pause.*) Is a sad ol place dis! De ol town, yeah! Nine peeplah inall, cludin dat bar keep. Big dime steamer him. Marky. Marky. Hoy Marky! Dat a Tang Top?!

He laughs. RUNT *returns.*

Ta ta, girl. Some ol man, alco mos likely, he sit at da bar
lashin inta da spirit. He talk bouts Jack Charlton an a liddle
tear come to his eye when he says… Dinny Irwin… Roy
Keane! A fling a beer mat dat go Schmack! Roy Keane, I
know dat fella… oh yeah… madge him cry an cry… an him
ol-ler an all!

RUNT. Rea, Pig?

PIG. Oh yes. Roy a da Pullovers I used call him!

RUNT. Nancy was he?

PIG. Was ta me, girl!

RUNT. Wow!

PIG (*they toast*). To you, pal.

RUNT. To you, Pig. (*Pause*.) Got a gawk at dat postur, Pig! En
ter tain ment!

PIG. Tom Borrow evey, ol pal!

RUNT. Sad sad story! Boo hoo whoo!!!

PIG. Boo hoo whoo!

RUNT. Boo hoo whoo!!

PIG. Boo hoo whoo!!

They laugh. Big silence.

Da delly playin a show wid Terry Wogan. He watch dees
tings dat go all da wonky yeah. He's Irish, Terry Wogan.
Really funny! Real good show, delly fans! Top show!

PIG *looks at the telly and goes into fits of laughter.* RUNT
laughs too.

Les go disco! Les go wild one!!!!

PIG *and* RUNT *in a nightclub. They dance. They are well
gone. The music is loud.*

Jus me jus me jus me jus me jus me!! Oh yes!! Dis da one!!
Real soun set Pig swimmin an swimmin in da on-off off-

beat dat is dance! Beat beat beat beat beat thru da veins full a drink! An Pig he wee wee full a drink! Dis is sex-in-step to dat beautifull soun dat deep deep down thru me pump da danceflower. On-an-off da off-beat dat is dance, on an-off the off beat dat is dance Pig move alone bud ta da crawd too he belong a family-a-sorts is wad he make wid deez happysoun fox. Pump pump pump pump oh fuck my head ja luvly beat deep inta me an take me home ta beddy byes an pump me more to sleep soft an loss lost... an still yeah I feel da finish of dis real music. I let da music leave da soul...

Sound of a poxy dance tune is faded up.

PIG. Fookchaa!! Stoodent, in a?

RUNT. Lookalike.

PIG. All dat chit-chat, chit-chat, chit-chat... SHAT!! Pork's brightest oud der an whod a guessed, Runt? I men, look dat yoke!

RUNT. Pig poin ta a lanky skin an bone dress in da height a ration!

PIG. Jesus da hairy an Joseph!

RUNT. He nee Runt style help! His tapioca skin globby eyes an bum hole moud all sittin lax need a mooppy hair style long since gone!

PIG. Das pugly, hey Runt!

RUNT. Dem stoodent type got no soul! Style in't in it!

PIG. Das righ, girl!

RUNT. De men dey act like ol dolls, da ol dolls do up like men! No tuck an seamed, no press liedly wid da iron.

PIG. Like yurs truly, yeah!

RUNT. Like dancin bags a Oxfam, dey no shame! Shame!

PIG. All dis chat give me a fuck a da throat!

RUNT. Pine, Pig?

PIG. Ta ta, yeah! We rob all in sied! Every nigh purrmotion
   nied! A liddle Smurf all alone it sit! Poor liddle lonely ting!
   War da mammy war da mammy?

RUNT. I'm ja mammy!

PIG (*shouts*). Wat you lookin at??

RUNT. Tanks, pal!

They drink.

   I look a deez students yeah, I tink a all da learnin das goin in
   ta dem, I tink a da books dey do read all stack tall inside dem
   oblong heads, I tink a da exam an all, all dat A B C plus an
   minus F an all... an Pig...

PIG. Wad now ol girl?

RUNT. Wad do dey wanna be?

PIG. Dey wanna be der mams an dads a course!

RUNT. Wadda we wanna be, Pig?

PIG. Leff alone. Righ pal!

RUNT. Righ, Pig. Mu zack up!

Music begins. PIG *dances with a woman.* RUNT *plays the
woman.*

PIG. Ja wanna dance?? Make no odds! I take her up
   anyhowways! I wine my charm aboud da waste! She say
   sometin... I don no dat squeak too well. She food inta me
   though an soon she in dance heaven! Kiss da face, will ya!
   On da lips, want ya! Don pull amay, hah! Owney baba cry! A
   full mast in da kax Pig he ready to set sail! She cry all
   elploss. I like ta lick da neck, yeah! Jus like a big lolly! She
   pinn close! Ohhhhhhh now look a da liddle titsies! Who da
   baba cry? Was jar name, lover?

RUNT. Liddle baby tiny tears?!

PIG. She's a terrible tease, hey Runt?

RUNT. Two Hail Marys an' an Our Father, hey sister! Les do da
   piggy dance, ya on!! War da fook is my man so!!

PIG. Ah pik da fucker, Runt!

RUNT. So Runt move in on misty mothball! Da tapioca king is who we'll take! Up reel close! Da boy he dead ugly okay! He got stoopid all ova him. Da liddle chalky face an tacky eyes. So on-an-off da off-beat dat is dance we move... me an dineasaur Barney, dat is. Da boy dance like a baba who nee ta piss o jus done a piss an nee ta leave! He stick a sweety han onta my neck an mamble a squeak I don understan! He sway-in an ova, da moud come-in like a gian manhole. An den he...

PIG. Den he kiss Runt! An dat my cue! Ova I move! Move real fass, yeah! Scream ou loud I scream an grab da liddle fuck an Runt she say,

RUNT. He kiss me, Pig! He gay me tongue an all, ya dirty-doggy!!

PIG. An Runt she nee an Oscar for dat, yeah, I almos give a liddle applause an all but da boy he say,

RUNT. Sorry boss! Hands off look!

PIG. But da damage it is *done, ya bad boy*! Oud a da door a dis poxy disco an oud onta Stoodent Straight I trow dis streaky stretch a bad bacon! See I play da par a da boyfriend, soap opera fans! Is jealous all ovur, in it! Smash! Ya fillty bollix! Smash smash smash smash smash smash smash smash!!!

PIG *beats him up*. RUNT *cheers him on for a bit*.

Goo fun, hey! Nice trick, cat woman!

RUNT. Birrday present in it?

PIG. Jar my bird day giff in life, Runt!!

RUNT. Pig the chrissy cracker! Bang bang bang bang!!

PIG. You're the one sweet ting!

RUNT. Better be better be!!

PIG. Jarr my bes pal in da whole whirl.

RUNT. Jarr my life, Pig.

PIG *grabs at* RUNT *and kisses her. She struggles and pulls away. A moment.*

PIG. Way da buzz go hun?

RUNT. Dis place pox. Les go eat yeah?

PIG. Burger baps-a-go-go!!

RUNT. Lead da way fas-boy!!

PIG *and* RUNT *in a burger place.*

PIG. Mister Kung Fu! Two Battur burgurs! Two Sauce! Two Chips! Two Peas! Two Tanora! (*Pause.*) An two fawks, Gringo!

RUNT. Our two mams all sweety an stinkin a new born babas n' blood! I member open an look my eyes an ja see a liddle baba in the nex bed. An dat liddle baba he look righ inta me, yeah. Our mams all da full of happy but da new babies say an do no-ting. We look cross da liddle-big space tween da beds… I see own him an he own see me. Deez liddle babies need no-ting else. So off home we go all packed! An da baby houses side by side la!… an birrday in birrday out… us togedder. An peeplah call me Sinead an call Pig Darren but one day we war playin in da playroom be-an animols on da farm an Darren play da Pig an I play da Runt! An dat wuz it! An every beddy time our mams pull us away from da odder one. Say night to Sinead, Darren. But Pig jus look ta me an ans – (*Snorts an oink.*) An I noel what he mean. So we grow up a bit at a dime an all dat dime we silen when odders roun. No word or no-ting. An wen ten arrive we squeak a diffren way den odders. An da hole a da estate dey talk at us. Look nasty yeah. But me an Pig look stray at dem. An we looka was happenin an we make a whirl where Pig an Runt jar king an queen! Way was goin down in dis clown-town is run by me an Pig fun fun. An Pig look cross at me jus like he look when we were babas an he alla say Les kill da town, ya on? An I alla say – Corse I'm on – I'm ja pal, amn't I? An liddle tings we do like robbin an stealin is a good ol feelin, yes indeedy. An we read dem buuks on howta figh da peeplah ya hate. An Pig own has me… an Runt own have him. But we make a whirl dat no one can live sept us two. Bonny an Clyde, ya seen da movie! Fannytastic, yeah! (*Laughs*.) But ya know, we liddle babas no mo. Is all differen. All of a puddin, ders a real big differ-ence.

PIG. I'd grobble all da Battur burgurs in China sept I'm struck in dis grubby tub, hey Runt!

RUNT. Say again?

PIG. I'd grobble all da Battur burgurs in China cept I'm stuck in dis grubby tub!

RUNT. Yeah! Course!

PIG. Wa do dey call Chinese takeaways in China, Runt?

RUNT. Don no!

The two sit in silence for some time. Eating.

PIG. Up up up up up up up up!!

RUNT. Off homes, yeah?

PIG. Not off no! Not off but out Runt!! Not off but more more more much more!! Sa out da door an da liddle ones step out onta Patsy Street! (*Calling out*.) PORK!! Cheerio ol pal!!

RUNT. Pig?

PIG. TAXI!!

RUNT. Purr us, Pig!?

PIG. We're da reel ting, ol girl! Les split dis party, yeah!

PIG *and* RUNT *in taxi.*

Crossheaven! Drive on, mister cabman!!

Sound of a car.

RUNT. An off we do!

PIG. Now das reel class!

RUNT. Look how da scummy wet grey a Pork Sity spindown da plughole.

PIG. As da two speed on, an on we speed! Sa so long to dat sad song, hey Runt!!

RUNT. Up an out ova da valley, Pig!! An da black a da cuntry like a big snuggly doovey it cuddle us up reel good, yeah!!

PIG. Snuggle down outta town!!

RUNT. Hey da fresh air, pal!!

PIG. Wine down da windy an drink it all in, Runt!

RUNT. Da taxi so fas dat da fresh air fill me up like a big happy ba-loon!!

PIG. Not like da stenchy piss dat we all know!

RUNT. Look a da moo moo look!!

PIG. Was me ol mam doin der, Runt!!

RUNT. Is way pass yer beddy times, ya silly cow!!

PIG. So fook off home why don jaa!! On an on, mister cabman!!

RUNT. On an on, an let da fas fresh air kiss an clean dis liddle girl up!!

PIG. Yer bird-day giff, Runt!

RUNT. Where Pig?

PIG. Taxi stop!

Car sounds stop.

Crossheaven, da colour a love, dis where it is hun!!

Sounds of the sea have been faded up over the above. The two look out.

RUNT. Nice.

PIG. Der ye are, pal. Das da big blue der. All dat wator, hah. Is all yers, Runt.

RUNT. Mine, Pig?

PIG. I got big bag in my plopet I can lash it inta. (*Laughs.*)

RUNT. Big open space an jus we standin here, Pig.

PIG. Like two specs a dust on da telly, hey girl.

RUNT. S'all calm dat move. Da sea dance up slow and down to up slow again. Is beautiful hey, Pig?

PIG. Top a da whirl, in it!

RUNT. Jesus, wad a smell!!

PIG. Salt. Salt sea smell.

RUNT. An da soun a da sea too...

PIG. Yeah, Rover at his doggy bowl, hey Runt?! Lap lap lap!

RUNT. I wanna walk inta da sea an neva come back. I wan ta tide to take me outa me an give me someone differen... maybe jus fur a half hour or so! Dat be good, wouldn't it, Pig?

PIG. Jesus, Runt! Dat be impossible! A half hour, fuck! (*Pause.*) I wanna huge space ship rocket la, take it up to da cosmos shiny stars all twinkle twinkle an I shit in my saucer an have a good look down on da big big blue. Derd be a button named Lazer dat blast all da shitty bits dat ya'd see, yeah. I press dat button an Lazer would fireball all below an den back down I fly to Crossheaven happy dat all das left a Pork Sity is my roam your roam an da Palace Disco cause das all dat matters, Runt... ress is jus weekday stuff.

RUNT. Da Palace Disco. Is a dream, Pig.

PIG. Pig know way da Palace is. Honest!

RUNT. Sure, Pig.

A pause.

PIG. Les go home, yeah. Beddy byes hun! Yer place furs stop, yeah!

RUNT. No race. Les stay.

PIG. Handsome.

Long silence as the two listen to the sea.

Happy birrday taday, Runt!

RUNT. Da bes', Pig! Til nex year, hah.

PIG *nods. A pause.*

Pig?

PIG. Yes, ol pal?

RUNT. Tanks! Is real nice dis.

PIG *and* RUNT *remain standing looking out at the sea. The sound of a car horn is heard.* PIG *looks over his shoulder.*

PIG. Fuck an wait, ja langer!!

RUNT *smiles at* PIG. *They look out. Lights fade to a new state.* PIG *and* RUNT *returning home. Music.*

RUNT. Say night to Sinead, Darren!!

PIG *oinks.*

Tomborrow evey, ol pal!!

PIG. Night, Runt!!

New state. PIG *and* RUNT *watching an episode of* Baywatch *which we hear under music. It's the next day.*

RUNT. Jees Pig, top a da delly dis!

PIG. God it all, pal!

RUNT. *Baywatch* da true winner, yeah!

PIG. Soun, sea an san

RUNT. An sex too, pal!

PIG. Da four 's'is, hey Runt! (*He laughs.*)

RUNT. Oh yeah! (*She laughs. Then.*) Look a dat boy! Bronze, he a blue-eye boy wid da real big beach balls, pal!

PIG. Imagine dat chunk doin da breast strokey on ol Runt, hey!

RUNT. Fook off you!

PIG. Imagine me gainst dat bloke in da race, hun! Who da winner den, pal?!

RUNT. Pig a corse!

PIG. Easy peasey bronze boy! Takey ye all on, ya Caliphoney babies!!

RUNT. Oh pal, look at dat der!

PIG. Nice gaff, yeah!

RUNT. Jiff clean, Pig! Da toilea bowl all a sparkly like is Jesus Christ's very own bog. Is beautiful.

PIG. Imagine havin a wazz in dat bowl!

RUNT. Oh yeah, pal! A pock-full a tens ta wipe da bum hole an all! (*She laughs.*)

PIG. Now das class, girl! (*He laughs.*)

RUNT. Imagine me born der?

PIG. An me too yeah! Two *Baywatch* babes, Pig an Runt!

RUNT. Hoy Mam! Wat time ya call dis, daff girl!! Dat da dins?! Runt she starve but who da you care, hey?!

PIG. Tateys an gravy, yummy yummy! Shlap it der look!

RUNT. Da fookin telly, Mam! Outta da fookin way, fatty!

PIG. Move it, maestro!

RUNT. Get da fook out so!

PIG. Don give up da day job, hey Mammy!

RUNT. Nice woon!

PIG. Ta ta, girl! (*Pause.*) Hey! Look a dat girlly there!

RUNT. Oh yeah!

PIG. Pamela Anderson!

RUNT. Beautiful. Beautiful girl!

PIG. But dat dress she wear, pal! It move like… like…

RUNT. Pig?

PIG. Like some liddle fedder ya can see fall in da sky oudda a birdy dat fly by.

RUNT. Ohhh yeah!! (*Pause*.) Eat up, yeah!

Music. PIG *stands out*.

PIG. Why I kiss da honey lips a Runt? An now all dat I put my gob to is Runt I take an tase. I close da eyes an see da inhide a Runt legs. Da silk a da tighs an da liddle heaven a panties dat sit above. Dat liddle furry tuff dat wid ma paws I cup an knead. Runt she get all sof an moise an she gendle press inta my han which seem to call her in… she come in. An we on da floor an lick da stiff tips a tits an all da time she on my fingur an da tongues dey disco dance an we move da wet spit aboud our face. I feel dis da time. Pig nee to be a man. I all caught up in da pants an zip zip Runt fold her han aboud me. She take me oud an me all shiny an hard I open her real sof. Open. She wet an moan. Liddle moan. I poosh an touch da way in. An now Pig an Runt are da one. We move an all is warm an sof wet, an da two well lost in da sex we move slow an gendle, yeah, an Runt she giv one mo moan an Pig he pour inta da Runt. We man an woman now. We kiss wid tongues. Pig go nice sof inside. My liddle baby seal wants oud. I kiss Runt eyes. She all shiny an glow as I pull-ou.

Music stops.

En ter tain ment! Ya on?!!

RUNT. Wat?

PIG *and* RUNT. En-ter-tain-ment!

RUNT. Now, Pig?

PIG. Off out yeah!?

RUNT. Wer da bobs so!?

PIG. A few bobs, Runt! Wat ya say?!

RUNT. Tonigh, Pig! Now?

PIG. Seventeen, yeah!

RUNT. Yeah!

PIG. Well les make up to flip out, yeah?!

RUNT *and* PIG. Up up up up up up up up up up!

PIG. Raceyaso!!!

RUNT. Fook yes!!

Sounds of Provo Bar faded up.

PIG. Hoy Marky!

RUNT. So back in da provo pub purr a secon nigh surprise yeah, an we in nee a da drink. Solids come in da shape of a scampi fries which Pig do hate but I do adore. So in da drinky fish mush my belly bubble an lisson as Pig wine up Marky an play da liddle bad boy! When all of a puddin

PIG. Get a gawk at that yoke! Is a fookin karaokee! Hoy Marky, was dis, boy? Charity funk or wat?!!

RUNT. It's a Cork Sinn Fcin do!

PIG. Say Marky, under another of his mam's *TANG TOPS*!!

RUNT. Wid dat da doors a da pub flap op an close as da Sinn Fein army pile-in an gadder bout da stout taps! Five hundred a da bas-turds all in nees of a good shave an da girlfrens like cocker spaniels come in oudda da rain! Da place go crazy!!

Sounds of extremely busy pub an somebody singing 'Danny Boy'.

PIG. Ere, shouldn't ya be out plantin bombs an beaten up ol ladies, ya fookin weirdos!!

RUNT. Fair dues, boy.

PIG. Pine, girl?

RUNT. Bag a scamp too, yeah!

PIG. So at da bar I mee da Karaokee-man himself of which I fine his name is Trevor. So Trevor, I say to dis small speccy spcc-a-fuck, how match a go, hey man!? Trevor say, it's free. Dat righ, Trev? Trouble is, says Trevor, only Provo songs tonigh, ol pal! Really, Trev? A fiver saw Trevor all righ for a surprise for my girl, yeah das her wid da packet a Scampi, a course she's nice, Trev-boy, she beautiful her!

RUNT. Oh get da fook off da stage, ape man!

PIG. Real lady, Trev!

RUNT. A crease ball wanders over. Da girlfren a Danny Boy it
   seem! I'll fuckin claim ya if ya don shift yer hole righ now!
   says she. I stan up. Smell da cheap fume frum way under da
   Martini. Her chip-paper skin wid drawn on eyes an lips dat
   lookalike well dangerous skidmarks. I face dis ugly puss an
   holdin a fist full a scampi fry I mash it inta her gob! When
   SHLAP!! (*Reacts to punch in the face*.) She pack a punch dis
   doll! SSMACKKK!! (*Reacts the same*.) Opens up da nose an
   blood all drip drip drop from da Runt! She hold hold a my hair
   an spit da scampi mush back inta my face an onta da fancy top
   I do wear. Dat stain won' shif too easy, I tink! FUCKKKKK!!!
   (*Reacts*.) Where Pig? Where ya now, Mister Kissy!? Mister
   Kissy! Mister Kissy! Mister kissy! Mister Kissy!!

   'Be My Baby' by The Ronettes comes on. PIG *performs it
   karaoke-style, miming to the original. Meanwhile* RUNT *is
   seen to be reacting to some violent punches to her face.* PIG
   finishes mid-song.

PIG. Runt?

RUNT. Outside, pal!

   RUNT *turns to* PIG. *Blood pours from her face.*

PIG. Wat mess! Look dat beat up face!

RUNT. Les ship out, yeah!

PIG. I fuckin burn da fuck who did dis! Who did, poin da way!
   Won' take long o no-ting! Justice see der face smash in!
   Who, Runt, who hey?

RUNT. No figh no more!

PIG. Lie back an die is dat da chant, Runt!

RUNT. Off home, yeah!

PIG. Is dis not Pig an Runt side by side remembers? A silen
   deal is wad we may way back in sain fridgets ward, we join,
   remembers, an in dat look we set out Runt, you an me pal, to
   make us king an queen a Pork Sity!

RUNT. Leave!

A pause.

PIG. Yeah ol pal, leave! Les leave all dat scum to dat scum!! An nows breed it in, pal! Breed in Pork's own poxy air. Elp sued da cut an bruise ya da have, Runt. Jees, Runt, wadda fook dat, hey! Sorry pal! Jus stay in real calm an Pig he put tings righ, hey! Smar boy!! So no tears liddle one!... please! (*Puts his hand over her eyes and covers his eyes with his other hand.*) Calm, Mother, calm! An sleep an res, ol sweet ting! Calm liddle pretty skin. (*Lowers his hands from her eyes.*)

RUNT. Oh my gian fuck of a beautiful white marbly mosque! Is da Palace. Is da Palace Disco.

PIG. Oh my guardy angel, ya come up trumps dis time, fella!!!

RUNT. How did dis big white house dat mus be da size a da Pork ferry ta poxy England, how did dis gaff play hide-an-seek purr dis long, pal? Is Pork dat big?

PIG. Not big no but manky. Not big, Runt, bud a big black barrel a black dat only do pause purr da pissy grey rain. Bud ya know, ol girl, even a great big poo poo has its diamonds an dis great big great marbly monstrosity which you did righly call da size of da Pork ferry, dis is Pork's own liddle gem!

RUNT. It take a Captain Cook like my very own bes pal ta sniff it out, hey! Wat a tresure you bot are! Dis is really it, Pig!

PIG. Oh no, pal, dis is much more dan it! Ya know where da top stops, well dis stop...

RUNT. ... is one step on top of dat top! Dis is like da cream cept beighy creamyer!

PIG. One hundred per cent don tell da true facs here, Runt!

RUNT. Dis is bettur den gold.

PIG. Da pick a da bunch!

RUNT. Champain,

PIG. Ta everyone else's Fanta! Man United,

RUNT. Ta everyone else's West Ham!

PIG. Ya noel wen Sonia finally become champion da wonder horse an gallop her way to suckycess bak in ol Goddenburg, yeah? An Sonia stan on da winny po-dium wid da whirl medal all a dangle from da pretty liddle neck as da nationalist rant-hymn blast da fuck oudda da sky an da green white an porridge all a flutter in da breeze. An all da Irish aroun da track an in da whirl, an anybod who even fuck an Irish dey all have a liddle tear a boy in der eye when dey say, dis is a great day for Our-land! Well Runt, dis is a bettur day!

RUNT. Fuck, yes!!

PIG *and* RUNT *go to enter the Palace.*

RUNT. Stop!

PIG *stops.*

PIG. Ah bollix!

RUNT. A gian cyclops a bricks wid bouncer tatooes on his toilea face.

PIG. Jus my luck, hey! So wers Hans gone, ol Chew-back-a?!

RUNT. Regular are ya?

PIG. Once in da moring an again in da evening, doctur!

RUNT. Pig too smart fur dis tic toc! Da man he screw up da face an lookalike a playt a mash an mushy pea sept a bit more starchey. He look down na Pig an he say, I think you know my little brother.

PIG. Who he, fat man?

RUNT. He worked down in the off-licence in Blackpool! But now he's on the dole.

PIG. Das a sad an sorry story.

RUNT. I watch Pig as da past tap em on da shold wid a hi-dee-hi. Offlicence. Blackcruel. Fuck me.

PIG. Yeah I noel Foxy, good bloke yeah!

RUNT. Bud da big man no who Pig is.

PIG. He place his shovel han onta ma head an den he say

RUNT. I hate the little bollix, myself!

PIG (*laughs*). Tank fuck!

Both laugh.

RUNT. Excuse me, so what's the password, then?

PIG. Sorry boss? Password? Is that wat you say, ol boy? Was da password, yeah?

RUNT. You know, what's the colour of love?

A pause.

PIG. Wad sorra love?

RUNT. The sort of love that you feel. The sort of love that only one colour can tell you about. The sort of love that can pick you up with a stupid grin cut ear to ear and can then cut your throat just as easily. (*Pause.*) An I look a Pig. An Pig he loss jus like da Runt is. Wad we know, hey? We all alone on da Palace Disco step wid Foxy's big pox of a brud. Seems like hours tic-by an Pig he jus look an stare straight ahead. (*Pause.*) An den, Pig, frum somewers he say,

PIG. Blue. Blue da colour a love. Is blue, yeah?

RUNT. An da big double decker in da pink dicky bow wave his kingsize han an say, Cloakroom on the left.

Music up. They're in. PIG *goes for the drinks.*

PIG. Pine, pal?

RUNT. G and T, yeah yeah!!

PIG. Ohhhhhhhhhh righhhhhh, hasta be, hasta be, Jo-Hannah Lum-mel-lee!!

RUNT. An a pak a Scampi Fries, Pig!

PIG. Three paks in dis side a heaven, girl!

RUNT. *Three* Pig!??

PIG. Dis a free cuntry, ol girl! Is yer want ta suck on dose liddle poxy fishy tings dat remind me a Nero's balls or sum schlop ya put out fur a liddle hungry kitty kat, yeah!! Runt ol pal, yer wish is my demand!

RUNT. My hero!

PIG. I fuck off so!

PIG *gets the drinks in.* RUNT *alone. Looks about.*

RUNT. So Runt she touchdown on all da chrome an da sky-blue Dralon! Who'd a guesst? Pig wid da righ ans fur Foxy's big brud an open sess me an Pig in a Cinderella ball, yeah, cept no sad old Billa or anythin panto, tank fuckin Jesus! Surprise surprise! Fur a sec I tink, hey mayb all dat drink drink play sum sorta shake it all abou insize my beautiful liddle head so I do da pinch an den da eyes all close den peep-op again an... an is true. Me in da Palace Disco!! Seventeen!!! All grow up! True story no fict!

PIG. Das three packs, yeah! Three! Fur da ol doll!

RUNT. All da beautys in here! All dancin good da on an off beat dat in real real dance! I spy sumthin begins wid Princess! She in black chambray dress fit an flare mid-calf, seamed. She know da fash! Real nice job! An I tink me as her dancin wid all da frens, yeah! All laughin, all dancin da same as one! Maybe we dress before in my room! Mayb we chit-chat an I say, I don fancy, Frankie, no, ohhh does it really show? An we all laugh an gozzel back another boddle a Ritz! No gozzel, no, sip! An we at da Palace Disco fun fun fun an jus maybe dis bloke dream cum true who look like Phil Babb or sum odder hunk mayb he say nice dress an I say, tank you, I made it myself an he kiss my han an not try to tickle my insize wid his Tayto tongue! Mayb dat be good! Mayb dat be good fun jus ta try, ya know!

PIG. Remarkable in it! I mean look at dat daycor, Runt, few bob der I'd say! Real class, all righ! Imagine dis yer gaff! Cept da prices mayb-a cheepur a course!

RUNT. Cheers, pal!

PIG. To you, hun!

RUNT. Who'd a guesst, hey?

PIG. All fur one!

RUNT. Yeah das righ. (*Sees something in front of her.*) Ders a mirror look!

PIG. Who dat beautiful pair?

RUNT. Us a course!

PIG. Like a misty an misses, Runt!

RUNT. Zact same. (*Pause.*) An Pig an Runt sit in da big bubble dat is my life! Seventeen years an fuck all chane. Pig still look ta me an dat look keep me in Pig-step! Runt da real runt in dis liddle carriage. Well, up up up up up up up up up up up up up up up, get up girl! Is yer choice, party girl!!

PIG. Was dis!?

A pause.

RUNT. Toilea.

PIG. Ja wan more a da Scampi ta soak it all up?

RUNT. Tanks bud no tanks.

PIG. Maybe up latur an show off da piggy dance, ya on?!

RUNT. Maybe, yeah!

PIG. Handsome!! (*Pause.*) An Runt off, leave da Pig in wat be a well ol feelin, yah yah! See I wan da buzz, yeah! Look les stop all dis chitty chat shat an les sees whos da number plum aroun here! Dey all look an laugh a me! Hear dem?!! I can see it, yeah! Dey loads a cash an look a Pig an, who he, dey say! Who'd da liddle boy in da a confirmation suity?? Well, Fuck anuff! I all calm fur *she* know who, but no more! Dis no me, no!! Pig he wan ta balance it righ an da Palace Disco need a less an Pig he da real teach tonigh, all righ! So who da furs hey?

RUNT. Tank you, I made it myself!

PIG. Was dis! Oh yes! Jus like before, yeah! Good ol Runt! She play da girlfren an misty Pig he play da boyfren! But dis time I read da message purr real! She wan *us* purr real! Me an her! We jar it! We fucking jar ya know!

RUNT *holds out her hand which we imagine is being kissed.*

An thru da pump pump pump a da disco dance I see it all! Pig on his marks an all set as misty hansome move in on Runt an

RUNT. Kiss my hand.

PIG. An das my cue!!! Ova I move! Move real fass, yeah! Scream ou loud I scream an grab da liddle fuck an Runt she say,

RUNT. Jesus Pig no! No!!!

PIG. Oud oud oud oud oud oud OUD OUD OUD!!!!!! Take oud! Move oudda da fuckin way! Door open shut! Throw! You dirty liddle fuck she my girlfren bollix! Smash! Kassshhh! Open da nose da eye! Blood blood blood! An Smashhh smasshhhh smash! I am da king ya fuckidy fuck! Ashtray! Smash kaasshhhh head smasshhh! Head crack op! She mine, luvver boy! She my girl! Me an her, king an queen ya bad boy! Scream baby liddle baby scream an SMASH SMASH SMASH... SMASHHH!!!!!

RUNT. Oh fuck.

PIG. Dead hun, jus like an action flic! Big mess dis!

RUNT. Cheerio. So-long pal.

PIG. Wat? Stay! (*Overlapping.*) STAY STAY STAY STAY STAY STAY STAY!!!!

RUNT (*overlapping*). GO GO GO GO GO GO GO GO GO!! An Runt race good dis time! Mus ged away! No mo all dis play an pain! So so-long to all dat pox! Go girl! Leave! An it well ovur, drama fans! Runt race her ways up da piss-grey straight wid da Palace Disco an poor ol Pig on her back! Jus me! Jus da liddle girl all aloneys! An still I see Pig like he besie me, yeah. He my one an only, he da bes an da worse pal in dis bad ol whirl. An I wan Pig an I wan for all da buzz an all da disco we do dance but hey ho an wadda ya know I wan fur sumthin else! Sumthin differen! Sumthin differen! Fuckin freedom!! Jus me!! Jus da Runt!! So mayb ta Crossheaven, mayb das where a girl can sleep sleep sleep an be alone. Jus me an da big big colour blue. Dat colour blue! (*Pause*.) An Runt take a breeder on Christy's Ring... an I look a da sun creep up on my pal Pork... *Cork*. An da sun it really is a beautiful big thing. (*Pause*.) An Runt she alone now. But is okay now, is all righ. (*Pause*.) Runt, she calm, calm down... an I watch... da liddle quack quacks... I look... at the ducks... as they swim in the morning sun... in the great big... watery-shite... that is the River Lee.

Where to?

Light slowly fades down on PIG *until out.*

Then light slowly fades down on RUNT.

Blackout.

The End.

misterman

This new version of *misterman* was first performed at the
Galway Arts Festival, in association with Landmark Productions,
in July 2011. The cast was as follows:

THOMAS MAGILL   Cillian Murphy
MAMMY'S VOICE   Marcella Riordan
EDEL'S VOICE   Alice Sykes
OTHER VOICES   Eanna Breathnach,
                                 Niall Buggy, J.D. Kelleher,
                                 Simone Kirby, Mikel Murfi,
                                 Morna Regan, Eileen Walsh,
                                 Barry Ward

Director   Enda Walsh
Designer   Jamie Vartan
Lighting Designer   Adam Silverman
Sound Designer   Gregory Clarke
Composer   Donnacha Dennehy

Characters

THOMAS

SIMPLE EAMON MORAN (*voice-over*)

DWAIN FLYNN (*voice-over*)

MRS. O'DONNELL (*voice-over*)

MAMMY (*voice-over*)

BILLY (*voice-over*)

MR. MCANERNY (*voice-over*)

MRS. CLEARY (*voice-over*)

TIMMY O'LEARY (*voice-over*)

EDEL (*voice-over*)

Pre-show and we're looking at an abandoned depot/a dilapidated factory. The space immediately feels inhabitable and dangerous with electrical cables everywhere. And yet dotted about it are small tiny 'stages', pristine in comparison to the surrounding debris. It suggests that someone is trying to live and has lived here for some time.

The lights go down and fade back up.

A thirty-three-year-old man is standing in the space facing us out of breath and sweating. This is THOMAS. He has a small sliced pan under his arm. He stands upright and opens his hand. He's holding a chicken's egg. It's a little dirty. He must have taken it from a chicken coop.

A dog can be heard barking outside the space. THOMAS looks towards it.

Suddenly Doris Day can be heard singing 'Everybody Loves A Lover'. THOMAS turns startled. He walks quickly towards a tape recorder and picks it up. He hits the stop button but nothing. He unplugs it from the back but the song continues. He takes out the batteries but there's no stopping Doris. He places it down on the ground like it was a bomb. He must try to ignore it. This is most unusual.

The song continues as he walks into the kitchen space he's made for himself where he has a gas stove. He breaks the egg into a little saucepan, adds some margarine and leaves it there on a low heat. This bloody song.

He walks to a small basin with water and soap. He vigorously washes his face and hands.

When he finishes this he leaves there and walks back and stands looking over the wayward tape recorder and Doris. He's got an idea.

He walks quickly to the back of the space, bends down and picks up something. He walks back towards the tape recorder holding a hammer. He smashes it down on the tape recorder. The song skips back to the very start and remains intact.

THOMAS petulantly screams with frustration.

He covers his ears but can still hear it. He has some tissue in his hands. He tears it up and shoves it in his ears. It's no good. He takes off his jumper and wraps it around his head covering his ears. Still no good.

He smells the egg cooking and returns to it fast. He turns up the heat and vigorously scrambles it. He empties it on a slice of bread on a plate and places them on a table.

But still this bloody song continues. He's got another idea. He disappears momentarily to a small room at the very back of the space. Sounds of pots and pans crashing to the floor.

When he returns out of the room he's taped two dirty teddy bears over his ears. Perfect.

Happy now he walks back to the tape recorder and stands over it.

It suddenly stops. Fuck it.

He rips off his teddy bear mufflers and walks up a stairs that leads to a crumbling platform. Up there he sits behind a table with two reel-to-reels on it.

THOMAS. Hello everyone!

He turns on both machines and gets to work.

We hear the voice of Simple Eamon Moran.

SIMPLE EAMON MORAN ON TAPE. Aren't ya talkin' to me anymore? Why'd you run away from me garage…? …. no need for it.

THOMAS fast forwards it and stops it.

SIMPLE EAMON MORAN ON TAPE. …and will ya be goin' to the dance in the school hall tonight, Starsky?

THOMAS fast forwards it and stops it. We hear the voice of DWAIN FLYNN.

DWAIN FLYNN ON TAPE (*screams*). Are you recordin' this? Once more for the record? You're not fuckin' wanted...!

He fast forwards the tape again and stops.

DWAIN FLYNN ON TAPE. And don't ever stand there!

THOMAS stops the tape. Stands and looks to a spot beneath the platform. He impersonates DWAIN.

THOMAS. And don't ever stand there!

He spits.

Good!

He sits and fast forwards the tape. He stops and plays it. We hear the voice of MRS. O'DONNELL.

MRS. O'DONNELL ON TAPE. ...and maybe it's best you went home.

THOMAS. Yes!

He's found what he's looking for. THOMAS rewinds it and stops. We hear more of MRS. O'DONNELL.

MRS. O'DONNELL ON TAPE. You've takin' things too far. Jesus look at your face—there's still blood—you need help, Thomas. Don't be goin' inside the Hall. Maybe it's best you went home, love.

THOMAS stops both machines and stands up. He pauses and looks down at them momentarily.

He places the chair in a definite position. He then takes a tape recorder in a canvas sling and puts it over his shoulder, securing it to his belt like a holster.

Carefully he places a cassette tape in the machine. He pats it gently.

Quick now and THOMAS comes back down the stairs.

He walks over to a loud speaker on the wall and takes the microphone.

He covers his eyes and...

Blackout.

In the darkness THOMAS is heard, his whisper amplified.

THOMAS. It all began from a Nothing. This loud crashing all began as a whisper… but a whisper that was from God, from Him, from the Lord our Master… and that whisper grew and grew and became this growling and soon a thundering and a roaring that was never heard in the Nothing before. And out of the noise came a voice, the great voice of the Lord and He said 'Let there be light'… and on the Nothing a light shone. And what was the first light like?

Lights slowly come up on all the small playing areas dotted about the space.

The light made the Nothing a Something which the Lord called Night and light was called Day. And He made the Earth and separated dry from wet to make the land and the sea, and He made vegetation and fruit and trees and covered the land in all colour and shone a bright yellow star to make the trees and plants grow. And then a universe of smaller stars and other planets he set turning in the speckled light. And animals of all kinds and shapes they ran about the Earth and swam in the lovely blue seas that as a child I too would swim in. And God made us, Daddy told me. Man and Woman in his likeness to keep watch on what He had made. To be watching. To be always watching. To be good.

THOMAS is fully lit now, his hands lowered from his eyes as he talks into a microphone.

But Man and Woman's soul was not like God's soul because it was good and evil. And evil it grew. It grew like that very first whisper but a whisper now of crying and suffering and it grew and is growing. And I'm watching… because more people fill the Earth and only some little good and some little happiness is found. Because Man has forgotten God's words He gave us in Eden… and His son we crucified Him, we killed Him for offering us kind redemption and just carry on and on and on and sin has become our religion, greed our communion and Evil… Evil is our God.

He looks upwards.

THOMAS (*whispers up*). Everything is not good, Daddy. (*A pause*) Daddy?

He looks up at a light blue suit hanging from chain that stretches all the way to the ceiling.

He then looks at his watch.

THOMAS. 4, 3, 2, 1. Mammy!

He turns on the reel-to-reel on the table. MAMMY is heard from it.

MAMMY. A scrambled egg is awful, Thomas? You used to take them boiled. What's the matter, my best boy in Ireland?

THOMAS. Tomorrow they'll be boiled again, Mammy. It's like eating yellow spit off a soggy bit of toast.

MAMMY. Stick with what ya know!

THOMAS. True enough Mammy.

MAMMY. Something I learnt when I traded the Milk of Magnesia for those Gaviscon tablets. God, d'ya remember that?

THOMAS. Yes I do unfortunately.

MAMMY. Jaynee I ate that many tablets that day I ballooned into the size of a whale only to expel myself in the evening for a good two hours.

THOMAS. There's a great honesty to Milk of Magnesia.

MAMMY. Milk of Magnesia's been clearing out foreign bodies for decades, hasn't it? It's like the United States of America of stomach medicines.

THOMAS and MAMMY laugh like fools.

THOMAS. I thought I might visit Daddy at the cemetery. I got some blue lilacs and lined the rim of the grave. I got a new bit of that gravel green stuff as well and I made a map of Ireland with the green gravel. It looks like Ireland drowning on the grave with the terrible sea surrounding it.

MAMMY. Oh that's nice! I think it's great you like flowers, Thomas. It's a nice side to your character.

THOMAS. It is, isn't it.

MAMMY. Are we all right for gas, Thomas? How's the canister?

THOMAS. The canister's fine, Mammy.

MAMMY. It's a little damp in here though...

THOMAS. Well that's the dampeness for ya!

MAMMY. A certain draftiness too.

THOMAS. There's a damp and certain drafty quality, all right.

MAMMY. There's no shifting it, is there?

THOMAS. No, there's no chance of that.

MAMMY. "There's only living with it." That's what you always say, isn't it Thomas?

THOMAS. Well who knows... might be blessed with a winning Lotto ticket... then you can buy all the gas canisters you want Mammy. You could fill this whole room with that many canisters it would be like waking up in the Bahamas.

MAMMY. Ohhh that would be nice.

Finishing his eggs. Closes his eyes and says a short prayer.

THOMAS. Lord watch over your humble servant keeping his soul clean, his spirit strong, through Christ our Lord, Amen. Right... best make a start!!

MAMMY. You might give me a rub with the Vicks when you get back from your travels?

THOMAS. I heard you coughing all night, d'ya know. It's not too good, Mammy. Like an old engine. Chugging away there, good style! Like a steam train, Mammy! Like a little old choo choo!!

MAMMY (*laughing*). Oh a little old choo choo!

THOMAS. Like a choo choo train from the olden days!

MAMMY. Choo choo! Choo Choo! Choo Choo! Choo Choo! Choo Choo!

THOMAS. That's enough now! I'll give ya a rub down later on, Mammy… don't you worry about that.

MAMMY. Off with you then, Mister Traveller. Get me a surprise from Centra, Thomas. A sugary surprise, Thomas. You know, what I like, love.

THOMAS. Oh I know what you like. Bye now, Mammy.

He hits the play button on another reel-to-reel. He unlocks some invisible locks on an invisible door. The sound of the outside world from the recorder.

THOMAS 'steps outside'.

Car.

The sound of a car.

Dog.

The sound of a dog.

Billy.

BILLY ON TAPE. Howya Thomas!

THOMAS. Hiya Billy! *(Slight pause)* I feel the front door's gentle shove behind me as I step out into Inishfree. The Lord God at my side… the day open and big!

He adopts a suitable voice for Mrs. O'Leary.

'Oh the cold Thomas!'

Are ya full of the cold, Mrs. O'Leary?

'Once I get the cold into my body it's very difficult to get the cold out, Thomas. Try as I might the cold just sits inside and won't budge an inch. And you love, going out for your "lil walk are ya?"'

I am! Off out for, Mammy, actually. Got to keep her in the biscuits.

'Oh she loves her biscuits, doesn't she!? She's mad about them biscuits!'

She loves her biscuits all right.

'A Demon for the bickie, ya'd say!'

Well not exactly a 'Demon', Mrs. O Leary, ah no. There's a lot of contemplation that goes with old age. No harm that this quiet solitude is accompanied by the occasional Jammy Dodger.

'You're a fine son to her, Thomas! Oh for God's sake when I think of my own son, Timmy!'

A slight pause.

Well what is it, Mrs. O'Leary?

'Well when I think of him with his disco nights and the way he'd bark at me like I was a black slave or something. "Mammy", he would shout! "MAMMY!" Like an old hound he would bark at me, Thomas. And I'd crawl in. Crawling into his bedroom because of these bunions stuck on my feet. I crawled into Timmy's bedroom the other evening and I'm not having ya on when I say a bomb had been let off… and then the smell, Thomas… well what with the bomb and then the smell…'

My God, was it terrible, tell me?

'Terrible isn't the word, Thomas! Beyond terrible! And he's sat there on his leaba like some lord, eating a large bowl of Sugar Puffs and playin' that awful computer game. I was scrubbing his room for days with my hands torn to shreds by the Harpic. Sure look at them!'

Well that's not on, Mrs. O'Leary! That's not on at all! Sure who brought us into the world only our Mammys… 'Children be obedient to your parents in the Lord'… that is what uprightness demands.

A sound of a car horn. THOMAS gestures a hello.

If you can't wake on the Lord's day and tidy away the odd pair of underpants, if it is not in your spirit to say that the spuds were lovely and that the meat was tender… if your parents are reduced to crawling around the house with callused feet well in my book you're not even fit for pig fodder. Look you send Timmy around my way and I'll have a word in his ear.

A pause.

'D'ya know what I'd do if I didn't have my senses?'

I don't, Mrs. O'Leary.

'I'd kidnap ya, ya little treasure!!'

Ahhh now, Mrs. O'Leary, stop it!

'(*Wistfully*) No I would, Thomas. That's what I'd do. The guards would have to lock me up for kidnappin' ya.'

God bless you Mrs. O'Leary and don't you worry about Timmy.

He does a gesture to say goodbye to her but it's not right.

No!

He does the line again.

God bless you Mrs. O'Leary and don't you worry about Timmy.

He gestures to her in a new way. That's correct.

Better.

He takes out a small notebook and writes.

Timmy O'Leary. Cleanliness.

Adopts the voice of DWAIN FLYNN.

'What are ya writing? You're writing in your little book again? Are ya writing about me this time? Are ya reporter, is that what it is? Reportin' about the community dance in the school tonight. Thomas Magill the Inishfree Rovin' Reporter. Reporting to who exactly? Is it Denis Boyle? 'Cause he's a measly old fucker if ever there was one. The amount of drink I've had in there over the years! Hundreds I've spent in there—Thousands!'

Impossible to put a figure on it, I'd say.

'Last weekend I spent me wages on pints only for Denis Fucking Boyle to turf me out… for what says you? For fuckin' bad language he says!'

Well I must commend Denis for his Christian actions.

'You agree with him then?'

DWAIN smacks THOMAS hard on the side of the head.

I do agree with him whole heartedly, yes!

'Sure where's the harm in the odd "fuck" or the occasional "ya dirty old cunt"! It's not written in the Bible that ya can't say those words, is it Mr. Holy Man?'

Those words wouldn't be written in the Holy Book, no Dwain.

'Didn't they have those words in the Middle East?'

They did Dwain, yes! And worse words I'd say those Arabs had! The reason why those words didn't feature in the Bible is because our Lord would want us to operate on a higher plain... Dwain? Not for human beings the language of dogs, the language of the dirty mutt. At our disposal are thousands of words which we can throw together in various patterns and create all manner of wonderful text and commun...

'Fuck you!'

A slight pause.

'Did you hear what I said, you fucking queer! Fuck you and your fucking words!'

A slight pause.

'Put that in your little book, you fucking headcase! And don't ever stand there!'

He spits.

THOMAS watches DWAIN walk off. He writes in his book.

Dwain Flynn. Profanity.

THOMAS cues the dog Roger.

Roger!

Sound of little Roger barking.

Away Roger! Get away!

The dog wanders off. Sound of car approaching and stopping. THOMAS finds a chair and sits on it.

He adopts the voice of the gloriously pompous MR. MCANERNY.

'Dull ol' day, isn't it?'

(*Cheery*) Well it will brighten up hopefully!

'D'you think it will brighten up, Mister Weather-man?'

Well it might, Mr. McAnerny.

'I don't think it will, ya know.'

Well it might or it mightened, who's to say?!

'I'd say you'd be better putting your money on the "mightened". I'd say that's where the wise money's going, Misterman.'

Well whether it will rain or not… I suppose we'll see the outcome soon enough!

'Of course we'll see the outcome soon enough ya can always count on that one. That's the thing with 'time' you see. Wait around long enough and sure as eggs is eggs something is bound to happen.'

Mirror!

THOMAS adjusts an invisible side mirror on the invisible car.

'Ah surety really that circumstances will be what they weren't due to the passing of time.'

That's right!

'A fool would bet against "time" having no effect on an event of some sort happening at some point. The very certainty of "time" continuing and proceedings altering due to the passing of minutes is a profundity that we live with daily. In a nutshell, Thomas… "Time" changes everything. (*Slight pause*) Goin' to the Community Dance in the School Hall tonight then, young man?'

No—I wouldn't be one for the loud music, to be honest with ya.

MR. MCANERNY ON TAPE. So off on your little walk then?

THOMAS surprised and annoyed by the intrusion of the voice.

'So off on your little walk then?'

I'm off to visit the cemetery, actually.

'Your poor dad. Now he was great man. Great man. Best shop in town! What a variety! A selection! And for those days. I mean bananas are two a penny now, of course! But back then when your Dad was your age sure people would travel to see the variety. Imagine saying that people would travel to see a banana. Sounds bonkers but that's the truth. That's the world's truth!! "Travelling to see a banana. That's where we're off to! We're off to see a banana from the jungles of Africa!!" Word would get around of the soft yellow fruit that was selling in Magill's Grocery and lines… I mean lines of people talking and laughing over this funny old bendy banana thing and all the people with the bendy banana grin on their old pusses, laughing and giggling away like happy monkeys!'

Toto's Africa is playing on the radio.

'Oh yes!'

MR. MCANERNY turns it up loud.

THOMAS stands listening to it for too long. He blocks his ears and turns away, the song muffled and fading out.

I stop listening…

He looks up.

…and look up. I look up to where I want to be. Up there safe in the clouds and far away from Inishfree.

THOMAS imagines himself in Heaven.

I sit like an angel of goodness up here. Sit in the bluey white making me invisible. I listen to God's music soothing and piercing me with His goodness. No more the smart words of Charlie McAnerny draining the life out of me. My head now free and without pain. (*Pause*) I'm in a place where other's speak is like poetry too. A place where I belong. I see other faces surrounding me. Beautiful and kind they welcome Thomas. Angels all of us as we sit amongst the clouds. I have a look down on Inishfree. My town. (*Pause*) And I see its pure white soul being stained by the bad. I see the goodness being chased out of people's faces. I look how temptation is twisting its ugly way into my neighbours… like they were blind and playing at the gates of Hell they look. But the good angel will make it change. My bright light of goodness making the pure grow again. And God has placed His hand around my shoulder. And me and God smile and look down on all my good work. "It's going to be such a beautiful place, Lord. Such a beautiful place."

A pause.

Again we hear MR. MCANERNY from a reel-to-reel.

MR. MCANERNY ON TAPE. Got to be off myself. See you, no doubt, in time.

THOMAS takes out his notebook and writes.

THOMAS. Charlie McAnerny. "Immodesty".

Suddenly the reel-to-reel begins to chew up with different voices layered over one another making them intermittently unintelligible. THOMAS stands looking at it, pissed off.

It stops and clear as anything we can hear MR. MCANERNY talking with THOMAS.

MR. MCANERNY ON TAPE. I'm saying it for your own good, all right? Do you hear me, Thomas?

A slight pause.

THOMAS ON TAPE (*whispered*). Yes.

MR. MCANERNY ON TAPE. This behaviour has to stop. (*Slight pause*) Now if you ever need to…

THOMAS stops the reel-to-reel.

A sudden noise from outside the space. It's that dog whimpering and wanting to be let in. THOMAS screams at it to "Go away!" He barricades the door with a huge piece of furniture.

Silence now. The dog has wondered off.

THOMAS. Very good!

THOMAS races across the space to a new playing area as he goes over a line of Simple Eamon Moran's.

But they're creepy old places, aren't they Thomas?!

THOMAS turns on another reel-to-reel. The sound of birds twittering and the outside. He adjusts the volume but it goes to loud. He blocks his ears and hammers the top of the machine. It finds the correct volume.

He pulls back a large piece of plywood. Behind it is a structure full of crosses made out of cans of Fanta.

THOMAS grabs a handful of flowers, composes himself, and checks his watch.

4, 3, 2, 1. Gate.

The sound of a gate opening as THOMAS enters the cemetery to visit his Daddy's grave.

Hello Daddy, it's only me, Thomas. I just popped out to get Mammy the bickies—I thought I'd check in with ya. (*Slight pause*) The graves looking smashing, by the way! It's the best of the lot, I'd say! Hey what do you make of the gravel map of Ireland on the drowning sea? It's dynamite, isn't it, Daddy?! A good joke. A-one!

THOMAS kneels down at his Daddy's grave and lays the flowers on it.

So! Mickie-Joe-Goblin-McAllister's been banned from the Community Centre for life, Daddy. A physio woman from out of town had a weekend clinic for the elderly. There was all manner of crippled people queuing down the road to avail of her healing hands. I had thought of bringing Mammy but she said she'd feel very awkward about another woman feeling her up. Not so Mickie-Joe. Apparently he walked in, dropped his knickers, said he had a chest infection and might he have a suck of a lozenge.

A slight pause.

He's not half as funny as he makes himself out to be. In my mind he's just a grubby little midget with a very long name—though that can go a long way in Inishfree, unfortunately organ.

The sound of a church organ playing "Lord Of All Hopefulness".

Billy Traynor got himself a new car, Daddy! Who's to say there's no money in shovelling S-H-I-T! He's as proud as punch just like the fella on the Lotto ad! Hey, will ya ever forget the day ya caught him pinching the newspaper in our shop, Daddy? Ya gave him an awful hiding that day! He was in bits that night in Boyle's! Pouring the pints inta him to ease the pain! Billy's only an old thief anyway! Everyone knows that. No doubt he'll be at the dance tonight jangling those new car keys at the young girls, God help them.

A pause.

I really miss ya, Daddy. But I'm doing my best with it and I bet you'd be proud of the work I'm doing about town too. It's just funny not having the shop… and it being so quiet about the house with Mammy and me and Trixie. The swelling's gone down after the kittens, by the way. Mammy asked me to drown three of them and keep the best one. "Best to drown the lot", I said. Being an only child is tough… being an only kitten in a town full of dogs would be a terrible curse though. It really would.

THOMAS listens to the 'Lord Of All Hopefulness' moving through the air around him. He begins to sing.

Lord of all kindness, Oh oh Lord of all grace, Your hands swift and welcome, Your arms… they embrace, Be there… for my Mammy, And give us… to pray, Your love is in my heart Lord, at the break of the day…

THOMAS adopts the voice of Simple Eamon Moran.

'But they're creepy old places aren't they, Tommy? Gives me the creeps just working beside the thing.'

Oh Eamon! Well what's creepy to some, gives great comfort to others. Though Daddy's sitting upstairs with the Almighty, down here his grave and remains still nourish my soul.

'God he was a great man though, wasn't he?'

You wouldn't be able to call many people great but my Daddy was great, all right.

'And strong too! You wouldn't want to cross your, Daddy. He could crush walnuts with his little finger, couldn't he Tommy?'

"There wasn't a walnut safe in Inishfree", he used to say.

A slightly uncomfortable pause as THOMAS waits for an invitation from Eamon.

'Will ya have a cup a tea with me? I've got the kettle on in the garage.'

Well that's awfully Christian of you, Eamon!! Just... wait a sec!

THOMAS turns off the cemetery reel-to-reel, grabs a chair and quickly sets up Eamon's garage space. He turns on a reel-to-reel inside there. Sound of music.

'There's very little things as good as tea in my book. Sure tea is what's made this country great!'

He fills 2 cups with a 2 litre bottle of Fanta.

'And even if it isn't great, at least we have tea to help us through the terrible darkness.'

We do that. Tea's a great salve.

A big dog is heard growling.

Good Lord, that's a very big dog!

'That'll be Rufus, he's harmless him. Loves the rabbits but very good with the kiddies.'

Oh right.

'So grab a seat where ya can! Hope ya like your tea strong.
Me I like my tea like tar. Unless ya can trod on the stuff it's
useless to me, boy!'

Sure once it's wet and warmish it's no bother to me! Well,
Slainte Mhath!

'Go bhfana í ngrá linn,
Iad siúd atá í ngrá linn.
Iad siúd nach bhfuil,
Go gcasa Dia a gcroíthe.
Agus muna gcasann Sé a gcroíthe
Go gcasa Sé caol na coise acu
Go n-aithneoimid iad as a mbacadaíl.'

THOMAS has no idea what he said.

Oh very good. (*Slight pause*) My God, what a collection of
cars you've got here! But ya know Eamon… I can't see the
attraction in travelling at all! People whizzing around from A
to B and not spending enough time having a good look
around! Do you know what I mean?

'I don't Tommy but ya plan ta tell me all the same!'

Ah I won't go boring ya now, Eamon!!

THOMAS laughs. Eamon laughs. They laugh together.
THOMAS continues.

It's just… it seems to me at least… that people are filling
their lives with unnecessary entertainment when the Lord has
provided everything that is needed already right there on
their doorstep. If time wasn't always spent in life's fast lane
people would see the simple beauty of the Lord. Now you
know what I mean by that, don't you?

'No.'

Well don't you worry that one day you'll wake up and forget
about all what the Lord has done for you? That the sunrise
and the changing seasons won't surprise you anymore. We
were given such a great gift, Eamon and such a beautiful and

wonderful world to play in. It's this arrogance that some people have. This wasting of everything.

From somewhere THOMAS has found a hurley.

All the Lord wants is us to love Him as He loves us. To return His love and to love each other. Why is that so difficult, Eamon? (*Slight pause*) When the Lord is not the first thing in your life it is not a life. Love and respect the Lord God and Heaven will be your eternal home. It's that simple.

'You're a walking saint, Tommy! The whole town's saying it, by Janee!! No doubt about it but you're well touched?'

Touched?

'By the man Himself is what I mean?'

Oh right.

THOMAS has found a kindred spirit.

Well a prophet of God needs a following, Eamon. Look I understand that you've got your hands full here in the garage here and helping out with the hurling team at the weekends but I've always felt that you've understood... that you understand my work in the town here. . . that there's a bond, maybe, between us. If you were to work alongside me—now I would work you hard but fair. We would call on people together. Put right where there is wrong. Comfort where there is loneliness. God's work is tough but the rewards, Eamon, are so great, ya know!

'I'd have to talk it over with the lads in the hurling team 'cause I wouldn't want to take the Lord's work lightly. I'd put in one hundred per cent for the Man upstairs, you know that.'

We would be a great team, Eamon!

'We would Tommy! We would! Crusaders is what we'd be!'

Well exactly!

'Like Starsky and Hutch... except delivering God's Law, of course!'

(*Laughing*) Oh very good! Very funny, Eamon! Really great joke!

THOMAS laughs and hammers the hurley on the ground.

He cues Eamon on the reel-to-reel.

Eamon!

EAMON ON TAPE. Y'all have a hot sup, then Starsky?!

THOMAS. I will, Hutch! Lash it in there, Eamon!! Thank you. God bless ya, partner!

A very long pause as THOMAS and Eamon laugh quietly to themselves at their hilarious banter.

Quietness then as THOMAS looks around the garage.

The atmosphere suddenly changes as he sees something pinned to the wall.

Is that what I think it is?

EAMON ON TAPE. Ah don't be looking at that Tommy.

THOMAS. But that Eamon… that is filth. How any woman can strip off and allow that sort of… (*Slight pause*) And… and you? You get satisfaction from some dirty prostitute stuck to your wall! Well this is not good, Eamon! I took you as my colleague and not some sick pervert man! But guess who's been led on the big merry-go-round!! Who's the big eegit only Thomas Magill!!

EAMON ON TAPE. Sure where's the harm in a calendar?!

THOMAS. "Where's the harm?"!! Is it not Satan's Black Angel right in front of me then! Well stop the rot—stop the rot!! Before I know it, you'll all be at it! Let me out of here!?

EAMON ON TAPE. Ah Tommy, for crying out loud…!

THOMAS. My name is Thomas!! My name is Thomas! My name is Thomas! My name is Thomas!

THOMAS smashes up the garages as Eamon's music blares out. THOMAS runs from the space.

Dramatic light change as the music and THOMAS stop.

And I run! And run fast up over the hill and past the church! My good words sent burning about me. Inishfree once more all bad and diseased. My legs unable to climb to Heaven are stuck still in the Devil's land. In Sodom, good Christ! In Sodom! And run Thomas run! Turn back and see Simple Eamon Moran standing at his garage door… his eyes a piercing red, his ragged wings lit by fire!! (*Screams out*) Lord God take me by my hand and lead me out of this festering pit! This Hell!! Save me Lord and place me sitting by your side! Save me Lord Almighty!! Save me!!

A dog starts barking on the reel-to-reel.

THOMAS stops. He imagines the dog approaching him. He's terrified and slowly backs away.

The dog is faded up to very loud now.

AWAY FROM ME ROGER! GET HOME ROGER! GET HOME!

THOMAS freaks out with punches and kicking. He's killing the dog. The dog stops barking as he is knocked unconscious. THOMAS continues punching him.

THOMAS eventually stops.

Music here.

THOMAS stands upright. His knuckles are bleeding a little. He must have punched the ground. He washes his hands in the sink.

He walks over to a new space where a small table and chair are set up.

He disappears from view momentarily and we hear pots and pans crashing to the floor. THOMAS returns.

He walks back to the table with a clean red gingham table cloth. He carefully places it on the table.

He turns on another reel-to-reel.

He sits. Music cuts.

Sound of a quiet café.

It wouldn't be everyday that I'd give myself a treat like this one but today I'm having a cheesecake! Definitely! Mrs. Cleary's Café… the red chequered tablecloths all bright and breezy. (*Whispers to himself, barely audibly*) Cheesecake. Cheesecake. Cheesecake. Cheesecake. Cheesecake. Cheesecake. Cheesecake. Cheesecake. Cheesecake. Cheesecake. Cheesecake. Cheesecake. (*Louder now*) Cheese? And Cake? How anyone could think that a whisked bit of cheese with a broken biscuit base could set the baking world on fire… they must have been (*Introducing*) And here she is!! The Ban an Ti!

THOMAS spins up from his seat and grabs an overflowing battered kettle as Samba music kicks in. He puts on the voice of the sultry MRS. CLEARY

'Ahh Thomas but you're looking fabulous! What a rig-out! It's top, it really is!! Oh look at ya! Jesus, ya've grown up to be a fine looking fella! Best catch in Inishfree, I'd say! Ladies are ya all right for the tea? Yee are!! That's fabulous that is and isn't Mrs. Heffernan looking like a new model with her hair-do done up on her head like a hairy fairy cake, if there is such a thing, Thomas!! A hairy fairy cake? Not in my little café! Not on your Nellie oh no!! Wooooooo would ya look at his lovely neat feet! Stuck there in his little shoes! I bet you're a dancer, hey Thomas! I bet you're a dancer? Fred Astaire had feet the picture of those fellas! Grab a hold of Mrs. Cleary and we'll have an old waltz for ourselves!'

I've just come in for a cheesecake, Mrs Cleary!

'And you've no time for a dance with me!? Are ya shy? You're not shy are ya!? Sure that's a nonsense! Up and we'll have a turn around the floor! Tonight's the community dance, Thomas! We'll get in some practice and show the whole town in the School Hall, won't we?! We'll show those old codgers a little bit of Fred and Ginger's still going strong as ya like in sad old Inishfree. Of course it is ya little dancer!! Dancing dancing ohhh the little dancer dancing there in his dancing leprechaun dancing shocs!!'

The Samba music cuts.

Look if you don't mind!! I mean, if it's all right with you, I'd rather not dance here or in the Hall this evening, you know! I was just out on my little walk to get Mammy the biscuits and I've just called in for some cheesecake! I mean, if it's all right with you Mrs. Cleary I'd like a bit of your fabulous cheesecake. If that's all right now, Mrs. Cleary!

Not impressed and MRS. CLEARY wanders off.

Ya can't be allowed to be seen dancing in the Mrs Cleary's Café... least of all with Mrs. Cleary. Ya can never tell if the rumours are true but if they are there's quite a few farmers around Inishfree who've taken to the old whisked cheese and broken biscuit base.

THOMAS takes out his notebook and writes,

Mrs Cleary. Indecent.

THOMAS suddenly looks completely exhausted. He rests his head on the table for a good twenty seconds.

MRS. CLEARY ON TAPE. You're cheesecake, Thomas.

A real slice of cheesecake appears from beneath the table.

THOMAS (*brightly*). Thanks very much, Mrs. Cleary! Magnificent... magnificence!

As THOMAS eats his cake a conversation is heard on the reel-to-reel.

MRS. HEFFERNAN ON TAPE. ...oh a little ways down from the garage. It was lying in the middle of the road.

MRS. CLEARY ON TAPE. And whose is it?

MRS. HEFFERNAN ON TAPE. The O'Donnell's, I think.

MRS. CLEARY ON TAPE. Oh little Roger?

MRS. HEFFERNAN ON TAPE. Must have been hit by a car. It's dangerous there...

MRS. CLEARY ON TAPE. Oh it is, yeah. Oh the poor little doggy.

The sound of a door being opened and a bell sound. THOMAS turns to it.

Music.

Immediately he is mesmerised at what he sees.

THOMAS. And then something walks into my life. A vision
with pale skin and her eyes green. She smiles at me as her
dress blue brushes by my hand. By the back of my hand. I
feel the tiny hairs on my fist tickle and stretch out, ya know
the way they do. She catches my look sending me blushing
and turning away. An angel, Thomas! A real angel. Jaynee, I
feel weak all of a sudden. My back to her. Almost resting to
her. I feel ashamed then. Can't figure out why—her grace
and beauty, I suppose. So beautiful and pure. I listen to her at
the counter. The life in her voice. The ease and humour of
God's words. Only her words, sounding of Summer sunshine. (*Pause.*) And then I see Eamon Moran's grubby
hands… as large and gluttonous as that whore Mrs. Cleary.
In front of this angel everything is filth. Everything, Thomas.

*He tries to clean the invisible filth from his hands with the
table cloth.*

He suddenly looks up and she is standing beside him.

Hello. (*Slight pause*) Thomas, that's right. (*Slight pause*)
When did you arrive? (*Slight pause*) No I haven't seen you.
(*Slight pause*) Well I've been busy too. (*Slight pause*) Doing
my work that's right? (*Slight pause*) Yes, I'm doing my best.
(*Slight pause*) You've seen. Right. (*Slight pause*) Yes, of
course I'll follow.

THOMAS leaves with the Angel, the bell sounding again.

The music continuing.

She walks towards the girls standing at the corner. The dust
in the air, everything it glows. And Heaven has found its way
to our grey withered old town and turned it all to Techni-
colour. And those smart talkin' girls drop their stubby cigarettes and genuflect in front of her. They fall to their knees,
bow their heads and she lays her hand over them and turns to
me… and smiles.

He walks into the street and towards her.

And it's like I'm stepping into the bluey white of the clouds all over again but with her by my side now. And I'm seeing an Inishfree being altered by her hope. Goodness transforms and the Lord God unlocks a beauty inside all these people… and neighbours greet one another with kind words… and community and respect is made by her just being here. (*Pause*) "You will not be alone anymore, Thomas. Because today I will find you… and I will walk with you."

His eyes fill with happy tears.

Thank you.

He smiles.

And from beneath her blue dress… and stretching out in the warmth of a new afternoon… wings. She takes to the sky and Heaven-bound she turns back to me. (*Slight pause*) In vocation we are together, we are the same soul me and you, the same One, that same smile! But what do I call you, Angel?! (*Pause*) "Edel." "Edel." "Edel."

The music continues for some time as he watches her fly off.

The music cuts abruptly.

He does the nasty voice of MRS. O'DONNELL.

'And what has you all pleased with yourself? You should be ashamed. I knew when I heard it. Mrs. Cleary said it wasn't possible but when Simple Eamon Moran told me what you did out on the road. You punched him to bits. He's fucking dead, Thomas! Look at him! To see little Roger's body tipped on the side of the road like old rubbish. When my Marty hears what you've done he'll knock twelve shades of shit right out of you, believe me boy! Are you listening to what I'm saying you mad fucking eegit!?'

I am listening Mrs. O'Donnell but to be honest you're making very little sense! Sure wasn't it you're dog who took the first bite?

'But to kick the poor creature to death! Good Christ, man!'

Nobody is as sorry as me, Mrs. O'Donnell! But in fairness it was either my boots or the vet's gun! It made little difference! The poor doggy didn't have a bright future once he bit me, now be honest, did he? I'll take these Jammy Dodgers off ya now, Mrs. Pearson!

A packet of Jammy Dodgers drop from the sky into his hands.

Would love to talk to you, Mrs. O Donnell but just have to get back to Mammy!

A slight pause.

I watch Mrs. O'Donnell carry her wet tears down the road and disappear into the grey. And take a deep breath feeling my soul lighten and ease once more.

The sound of wind swirling.

And that's when it starts, ya know! Those grey clouds gather above and start to spin… and Edel starts spinnin' them for my entertainment! And she spins them so fast I feel almost sucked up by them! Like I'm being sucked up by a giant Hoover and sent to somewhere beautiful! Somewhere where me and my angel walk hand in hand! Somewhere good, Thomas!

Enormous sounds and music as THOMAS closes his eyes as his Universe spins around him.

The music and sounds continue for some moments.

They suddenly stop.

A voice on the reel-to-reel now. It's MRS. O'DONNELL.

MRS. O'DONNELL ON TAPE. … is it true though? Did you really kill him, Thomas?

The Samba music begins to blare out.

THOMAS ON TAPE (*whispered*). I don't know. I was on the road… I wanted to get away… (*He trails off. He can't talk*).

He smashes off the café reel-to-reel but the other reel-to-reel suddenly mashes up and distorts.

It fixes itself and the sound now of THOMAS running away and crying. THOMAS glares over at the reel-to-reel.

He walks to it and turns it off.

He goes to the sink and cleans his hands again. He dries them and walks over to the space where he's made his MAMMY's kitchen.

He puts on the reel-to-reel on the kitchen table. Sound of generic country music is heard from a radio.

He takes a can of Fanta from somewhere. He opens it and drinks it back. It's a well earned drink.

MAMMY. Welcome back, the Thirsty Traveller! Would you believe it but Trixie's in one of her moods again, Thomas!

THOMAS. Is she now.

MAMMY. I threw her a frozen Fish Finger to lift her spirits. She's been sucking on it like a fat cigar for a good half hour but you've never seen such a miserable expression on a kitty.

THOMAS. Right.

MAMMY. She's just not been the same since all her kitties got drowned.

THOMAS. Mammy I've told you those kittens are in a better place! You can't walk ten yards in Inishfree without meeting a hound. (*To Trixie*) Up Trixie, come on!

THOMAS holds 'Trixie'. A cat made of old jumpers.

MAMMY. They say a dog can sniff out the bad in people.

THOMAS. Oh do they now?

MAMMY. I read an article in Ireland's Own about doggy intuition.

THOMAS. Well sure it's no wonder the streets are riddled with dogs so, when you think of the terrible carry on in this town!

MAMMY. Oh very good!

THOMAS (*to Trixie*). Now Mrs. Trixie. 'Less you want to end up in my notebook, you need to change your ways, ya hear me now! Cheer up!

*THOMAS tosses 'Trixie' away. Sound of a cat squealing on
the tape.*

Time to take your top off, Mammy!

*THOMAS lifts up an enormous tub of Swarfega. He opens it
and begins to massage it into the table. We can hear
MAMMY groan for some time. She stops.*

The sound of swirling wind again.

The Vicks begins to lift little clouds of doubt that often
wander into my head. And I can see the happy destiny of
Inishfree being painted by me and the Angel Edel. It's all
beginning to turn. Goodness has found a new strength. And
so the change begins.

*THOMAS continues to massage the Swarfega into the table.
He stops and dries his hands.*

MAMMY. Thanks Thomas! You're a great little healer. Great
healing hands, God bless them.

THOMAS. Well you know, sitting over a gas heater doesn't
help your breathing, Mammy, I've said it once and I'll be
saying it a thousand times.

MAMMY. Oh but it gets awfully cold, Thomas.

THOMAS. I think you'll find that putting on some extra clothes
will sort you out there. It doesn't take a brainbox to figure
that one out, Mammy.

MAMMY. I'm sorry, Thomas.

THOMAS. All I'm asking you to do is throw on an extra
jumper. It's not like I'm asking you to fetch me a packet of
biscuits from the shop everyday.

MAMMY. All right, Thomas.

THOMAS. Look Mammy, I think a little more understanding is
needed here. I'm looking after both our interests. Your sore
cough and me wasting God's good time spreading the Vicks
on. I'm asking you to do something that even you could
manage, Mammy! A jumper, that's all! An extra jumper!
Give me one less thing to be worried about.

MAMMY. Oh I'm sorry…

THOMAS. I mean, do you have any idea of the day I've put down? And what now the Lord has bestowed on me! A little bit more co-operation would be appreciated! It would make my work a lot easier to come home to a happy home, Mammy! I'm not asking for much… but when I come through that door… what I expect… what I am looking for… is respect from you and Trixie. The same respect that you both showed Daddy…

MAMMY. Why Thomas?

THOMAS. Ahhh Mammy—you're not being very bright today, are ya? Do I have to spell it out to you?

MAMMY. Stop it, Thomas…!

THOMAS (*screaming*). You stupid woman! Have you under- stood anything I have said?! Just put on an f-ing jumper!

Music here.

Have you any idea of the cost of heating this room!? The f- ing gas bill, Mammy!! You will not ruin my work woman!! Are you listening to me?! Look—JUST DO IT!!

Dogs outside have started to bark, seemingly startled by THOMAS screaming.

THOMAS looks towards the metal door to the outside and shouts.

THOMAS. Come on then—HOUND!

He races to the door and smashes it with his fist. The dogs go crazy. THOMAS starts smashing the door and barking back at the dogs.

MAMMY (*crying*). What are we going to do now, Thomas? What are we going to do…

The music and the dogs swell. THOMAS turns back into the huge space he has created. A sudden power surge and the space is calling him back. THOMAS head drops as the music, dogs, lights continue aggressively.

*Suddenly he walks up the 'street' reel-to-reel and turns it on.
THOMAS's demeanour, bright and excited now as he opens
those invisible locks in the invisible door.*

*Music suddenly stops. The sound of the outside, the sounds
of a bright summer's day.*

THOMAS. Car.

The sound of car.

Dog.

The sound of dog.

Billy.

BILLY ON TAPE. Howya Thomas.

THOMAS. Hiya Billy. (*Slight pause*) I feel the front door's
gentle shove behind me as I step out into Inishfree. (*Slight
pause*) I look above and I see a bright light cut through the
clouds. See her wings split the air. And she's coming now.
She's here. (*Slight pause*) Hello Edel.

*The reel-to-reel beside him suddenly begins and the voice of
TIMMY O'LEARY is heard.*

TIMMY O'LEARY ON TAPE. All right, Thomas.

THOMAS. Well if it isn't Timmy O'Leary, the boy who treats
his Mammy like an old dog!

TIMMY O'LEARY ON TAPE. You what?

THOMAS. Slovenly behaviour will always catch up on a man,
Timmy. Only this morning I listened to a litany of exploita-
tion perpetrated on your little dote of a Mammy.

TIMMY O'LEARY ON TAPE. What are you talkin' about?

THOMAS. "What are you talkin' about? What's he talkin'
about?" Do you hear this Edel?! I'm talkin' about a sixty-
seven-year-old woman crawlin' about on her hands and
knees 'cause her feet are being eaten by bunions, Timmy!! A
woman who's Harpic poisoned hands have been mummified
into tiny claws! Those same claws have to scoop up soiled

underpants and toxic socks and all manner of fungaled food and all the time Lorded over by her sullied son!

TIMMY O'LEARY ON TAPE. Are you with him?

THOMAS. She is with me as a matter of fact yes but it's me talkin' to you, young man!

TIMMY O'LEARY ON TAPE. Right.

THOMAS. Right! thirty-two years ago the Lord God planted a seed inside your Mammy and gave your Daddy the direction and drive to water that seed and thus began your foetal life inside your Mammy's tummy. And she kept you there and no doubt gave you the proper nourishment a mother gives to her unborn child. She would have to endure atrocious heartburn, embarrassing flatulence, seismic swings in her personality but she endured all of this, Timmy, out of love. And when she pushed you out in the Regional Hospital there was probably not a happier woman in the whole of the county. And she brought you up, didn't she, and she watered and fed ya, and put clothes on your back and taught you how to read and write and introduced Jesus Christ through the catechism to you. She had hopes for you, Timmy! Happy hopes full of possibilities! And pictures, naturally, would form in your Mammy's head as she filed her bunions of an evening! Amazing happy pictures of her son finding employment and putting his stamp on the world! And there, under God's direction, he would find a girl and suddenly your mother is choosing her rig-out for the 'big day', the many hats she could choose, Timmy! And yet only moments into your adult life it's like you're shrinking the world around you! And for each second you're living like this you are mocking the world that God has created, you are standing on the dreams of your Mammy, you are denying her a son that she can be proud of—you are denying her fancy hats, Timmy!! (*Slight pause*) Now will you do me a favour and think of that the next time you stand in your dirty bedroom?!

A slight pause.

TIMMY O'LEARY ON TAPE. Think of all of it?

THOMAS. Like a gospel of faith, think of it.

A pause.

TIMMY O'LEARY ON TAPE. Okay.

A pause.

THOMAS. Well thanks very much, Edel. (*Pause*) Oh I do my best, you know. (*Pause*) Well to be honest I still believe this town could be great one day—all the nastiest words in the world couldn't turn me from my work. (*Slight pause*) I always had God as a companion. Could always see Him in everything and everywhere just like that first prayer book tells you, you know. I can maybe sound too strong at times but the quicker we atone for our sins the sooner the world will open with love and peace…

She has said something.

What's that…? Well yes… I'll go where you want. Just wait…

He grabs an old rolled up battered green carpet. He places it on the ground and kicks it out. It unrolls majestically.

A pause as he 'watches' her lead the way.

We walk.

Music here.

And it's like the first walk. And around us good neighbours stop and bow their heads and let us pass, their souls rising up to Heaven then. Walk on and curtains twitch but with no laughter now, a grace is laid out before us and people will talk of this day forever. Around us the shops and houses of Inishfree they slide beneath the ground and soon too the road falls beneath until all that's left is a blank horizon stretching on. And me and the Angel walk alone over a wilderness of dirt and lose ourselves in dreams of a better life. And there's only us in this world but already beneath our shoes a new grass begins to grow. And it grows underneath and spreads out over the wilderness—meadow of green and yellow crocuses pinging out of this carpet and stretching to a new sun in this new day. We walk on and about us an orchard pushes itself up from the earth. She talks God's words to me and about these words apples pop into life, ripen in moments and colour this green world with wonderful dots of red. How beautiful this new world is. How pure in hope, how free in dream. (*Slight pause*) And the past history of me and what I have lived through, the hurt, the beatings, the abuse, the lies... they evaporate in the air around me. And we will build anew her and me and it will survive past a week and into years and centuries and we will make new histories of hope and peace and love.

The sound of a river now.

The orchard sweeps down to a river and our legs take us there, our hearts' caught in anticipation. We find a clearing on the bank, the grass all soft beneath my hands and we sit and watch the blue-grey river moving past us.

He goes to 'her' and sits. A pause.

I can see her wings all folded and white and soft they look. (*Slight pause*) "You've travelled so far, haven't you Edel?" (*Slight pause*) And she smiles at me and stays quiet. We know what we are building. Our words have been said and now is the time to sit quietly in the Eden we've built.

A pause.

Her hand is stretched out on the grass.

A pause.

She's saying words I can't hear. (*Pause*) Edel... can I hold your hand?

Thunder and the sound of torrential rain. The stage and THOMAS are drenched in water from the fire sprinklers.

THOMAS stands up furious and hurt.

Not for the first time God roars down on Inishfree! I walk in the rain with its tracks pouring down my face and drenching my heavy soul. I hear someone bark and then laugh! Laughing at me!! Will I ever be free from those laughs?! Walk on Thomas!

Crash of thunder.

I'm feeling the whole town sit hard on my back and wanting to drag me down to their level. 'God saw that human wickedness was great on Earth and that human hearts contrived nothing but wicked schemes all day long. God regretted having made human beings on Earth and was grieved at heart. And God said, "I shall rid the surface of the Earth of the human beings whom I created—human and animal, the creeping things and the birds of Heaven—for I regret having made them." But Noah won God's favour. Noah was a good man, an upright man among his contemporaries, and Noah walked with God.'

Again a crash of thunder. THOMAS starts barking at the whole of the town. He stops.

I see some man outside my house with his thumb stuck to the doorbell, his face furious from the long wait and Mammy sat inside like the Queen herself! (*Laughs*) He turns and walks fast towards me, yelling about his dead dog Roger! It's me he wants, it's me he wants!! Oh Christ, please, no!! No No NO!! DON'T DON'T!!

THOMAS is struck on the face and falls to the ground. He splashes violently on the soaked ground screaming like a child.

Sound of Mr. O'Donnell screaming at him from a reel-to-reel.

MR. O'DONNELL ON TAPE. YOU FUCKING FREAK! TO KILL MY FUCKING DOG! YOU'RE INSANE, MAN, YOU HEAR ME! GET UP! GET THE FUCK UP AND FIGHT ME! FIGHT ME! FIGHT ME! FIGHT ME!

Rain and sounds continue for some time. Then suddenly stop.

THOMAS lies crying loudly on the ground. He stands and roars at the town.

We hear Doris Day singing the beautifully lonesome, 'Time To Say Goodnight'.

During the song THOMAS undresses out of his wet clothes to his underpants.

His body is heavily bruised and scarred from where he's been hurting himself.

He lowers the light blue suit towards him.

He puts it on. It's a little too big and we can guess that it's his father's suit.

The song ends.

MAMMY (*sighing*). Ohhh Doris Day. Sure that's Heaven there, isn't it?

A pause.

Doris Day did for baby pink what De Valera did for black, didn't she Thomas. She's a real beauty.

A pause.

MAMMY. I'd love to have a cup of tea and a biscuit with Doris. She doesn't look like a Jammy Dodger sort of woman but of course that's no reason not to like her. She's more of a Lemon Puff lady, really.

A pause.

MAMMY. How's the river looking Thomas?

THOMAS. As rivers do. Different but the same.

MAMMY. Ah that's good. Sure no news is good news.

A pause.

MAMMY. You're off out are ya?

A pause.

THOMAS. The Community Dance is on in the School Hall. I thought I'd show my face to them.

MAMMY. There's no point being locked up in here with your Mammy all this time.

THOMAS. Sure I don't mind that. I don't mind that at all, Mammy.

A pause.

MAMMY. You're so good to me. I love ya son. I really do.

THOMAS. I don't know what sort of creature I am without you, Mammy. It seems like I've nearly got it all sewn up in here. Almost. And if I wish it strong enough I can sort of see Daddy next to you on the couch watching the quiz shows on the telly… And I'd be sitting by his feet.

A pause.

Sometimes I feel that love's gone on holidays… that somehow it slipped out the front door to another place entirely, Mammy.

A pause.

I'll be home very late, I'd say. I'll be dead quiet.

MAMMY. You've something on your mind, Thomas?

THOMAS. No no. (*Slight pause*) Sweet dreams, Mammy.

THOMAS turns off the reel-to-reel in the kitchen. He kisses the table like he was kissing the top of her head.

He walks out of this space. He barely bothers with the 'locks on the door' He steps to the outside. The street reel-to-reel magically turns on.

The sound of a car passing.

The sound of a dog barking.

The sound of BILLY saying hello.

BILLY ON TAPE. Howya Thomas!

THOMAS. I feel the front door's gentle shove behind me as I step out into Inishfree. My town. (*Slight pause*) I look across the road as they queue to get inside the Hall. I watch Dwain Flynn relieve himself against our house and I think of me tomorrow on the cold hard ground scrubbing his memory away. (*Pause*) I watch Simple Eamon Moran chattin' to Timmy O'Leary ahead of me in the queue. Timmy looks at me and I watch him mouth the word 'Edel' and Simple Eamon laughin'.

A pause.

Then Mrs O'Donnell and her husband come over to join in. I watch as he replays my beating, doing the face of a crying baba. The face of Thomas. All I can see is the emptiness inside them. Their life scooped out from them. Now I feel... nothing for them.

A pause.

There is a town where angels from Heaven come to visit Earth. There's a great love between all men and women there. A respect, a kindness. Just a light warm wind is felt through the town as the river pops and gurgles with ease. There are no wicked tricks played. Words are pure. There's only goodness there.

Pause.

The queue begins its shuffle into the Hall. There's so much that has to be said to these people. And I feel God's strength building me up and holding my hand as I walk. . . walk into Hell.

Sudden sound of the dance as colourful balloons fall onto the stage. THOMAS walks in all hunched. Suddenly he has the confidence to do what he must do.

THOMAS runs up and fires on the reel-to-reel he was working on at the very start.

A huge cacophony of voices is heard—the voices of the people of Inishfree judging him, mocking him. This is mixed with the sound of people dancing to music. It swirls around like a storm.

THOMAS stands on a chair and addresses them through a microphone.

A hell of a day, hey everyone!? A hell of day! I say yee all had a good laugh down in Boyle's tonight, didn't ya?! Laughin' about me! All the chat about Thomas Magill and his mocky-a angel! Well it's me who's laughin' now, ya hear me! (*Slight pause*) Dwain Flynn and your filthy mouth... you Charlie McAnerny—thowin' shapes around town like ya

own it! I see ya both there! I'm lookin' at ya and you're
lookin' back at me, aren't ya?! None of you're dirty words
now Dwain! My words, Charlie! My words, Mrs. Cleary!
Shame on you! Mr. O'Donnell, the Devil's keepin' a special
seat for your backside! What you did to me outside on the
street?! You will burn in Hell for that?! It's me who's
laughin' now at you and your wife! (*THOMAS laughs*) The
rest of ya—I did my best! My very best but that is over! I
listened when no one else would listen to ya! I believed that
you could all do some good but that was before you tricked
me like a fool! Taking advantage of my search for love and
you tricked that girl too, didn't ya?! The Devil has had his
last day in Inishfree, make no mistake! A hell of a day for
him! (*Slight pause*) What are me and Mammy and Trixie to
you, hey? We are nothin'! When my Daddy died and we lost
the shop—you gave us no respect! You used us for all those
years and then dumped us aside like old rubbish! That's
right, isn't it?! Laughin' in Boyle's Pub, tonight, laughin' and
barkin' just like every other night! Stampin' my good name
into the ground and cursin' God like the hounds that you are!
You all recognise my Daddy's suit, don't ya?! My Daddy
would smash the lot of ya if he was here in this Hall! He
would beat ya senseless—and it's you listenin' to me!

*THOMAS quickly gets down, puts on a pair of shabby angel
wings and hops back up on the seat. He's suddenly more
focused now.*

And God said to me, 'Come back up to Heaven, Thomas!
Your good work has been ignored as was my son's good
work! Join your Daddy! Your Mammy will be saved for she
is the Mother of Righteousness! Leave Inishfree, Thomas!
Leave them to die!' And we will go up to Heaven and sit
with the Lord God and we will make a new house up there…
and I will forget you and that girl you sent to trick me! I will
start each new day and night with my soul clean, my heart
light, this town forgotten! It's too late to repent by the way. It's
far too late! 'For he who sows to his own flesh will from the
flesh reap corruption?' I am stronger than the lot of you and I
will watch you die… because you are not God's friends—you
are the Devil's friends! SO… HEAR… THIS… NOW!

THOMAS places the microphone against the tape recorder and presses the play button.

He presses the play button on the cassette player around his neck.

We hear the voices of THOMAS and the fourteen-year-old EDEL down by the river. She speaks with an English accent.

EDEL ON TAPE. Let's sit for a minute only 'cause I gotta get back. What's the time anyways?! You haven't spoken for a half hour! Somethin' up? Thinkin' about God and things? Hello?! Anyone in there! Right I really gotta go! I told the girls I'd be back by five to get ready for the dance…

THOMAS. Can I hold your hand?

A slight pause.

EDEL ON TAPE. No. Definitely not. Let's go!

THOMAS ON TAPE. Please Edel!

EDEL ON TAPE. Are you recording this?! The girls said you would! Let me see it! Come on! Give it to me!

She is heard grabbing the microphone.

EDEL ON TAPE (*shouts into the mic*). Hello Thomas!! Hello! It's me! It's Edel!

THOMAS ON TAPE. Give it back…

EDEL ON TAPE (*continuing. Pretending to be scared*). Someone help! Help—help me!

THOMAS ON TAPE. Stop that!

He grabs the microphone back.

EDEL ON TAPE. Fuck this, I'm off! Are you staying or what?!

THOMAS ON TAPE. I want to hold your hand, Angel!

He grabs her arm.

EDEL ON TAPE. OW! Don't fucking do that…!

THOMAS ON TAPE. Stay with me!

EDEL ON TAPE. You're hurting me…!

THOMAS ON TAPE. Don't speak to me like that!

EDEL ON TAPE. Let go! STOP!

THOMAS ON TAPE. Did they send you?!

EDEL ON TAPE. That hurts!

THOMAS ON TAPE. My God, have they sent you here… SIT DOWN!

EDEL ON TAPE. It was a dare, that's all! A DARE!

EDEL is heard being punched hard in the face.

THOMAS ON TAPE. Out!

EDEL ON TAPE. Oh Jesus no…!

THOMAS ON TAPE. OUT DEVIL OUT!

EDEL ON TAPE (*screaming*). NO THOMAS STOP! HELP! SOMEONE HELP ME!

THOMAS punches her again and again.

THOMAS ON TAPE. OUT! OUT! OUT! OUT!

A sudden horrific noise of the tape recorder smashing against her head.

THOMAS ON TAPE. Help me God… Help me…

THOMAS smashes her head with the tape recorder over and over and over.

THOMAS listens to it for some more moments until he's heard enough.

He stops the cassette player.

Silence.

How small he looks in this huge space.

He turns to an 'imaginary good angel' and tries so hard to lose himself back in the pretend.

THOMAS. And now good angel… I can kiss your hand.

He kisses the microphone.

Everything is so right here. Because nobody's listening. Nobody's listening. Nobody's listening. Nobody's listening. Nobody's listening…

For all his trying to escape his past… in the moment he knows the fight is lost.

His hand slowly holds the microphone out from his body. He drops it.

It smashes against the ground.

Blackout.

The end.

bedbound

bedbound was first performed at The New Theatre, Dublin, as part of the Dublin Theatre Festival 2000. The cast was as follows:

DAD   Peter Gowan
DAUGHTER   Norma Sheahan

Director   Enda Walsh
Designer   Fiona Cunningham
Lighting Designer   John Gallagher
Sound Designer   Bell Helicopter

The play received its UK premiere at the Traverse Theatre during the 2001 Edinburgh Festival Fringe, and was revived at the Royal Court Theatre Upstairs, London, on 10 January 2002, with the following cast change:

DAD   Liam Carney

Characters

DAD

DAUGHTER

There is a large box in the centre of the stage made out of plasterboard. Suddenly the wall facing the audience crashes to the ground. A light comes up on a small child's bed inside the box. It is heavily stained and grubby. On one end of the bed is a young woman. She is the DAUGHTER. *Her back is twisted and we can see that she is obviously crippled. Her face is filthy, her hair tangled and manky. On the other end of the bed facing her is her* DAD. *He is a large fifty-year-old man. He wears a suit which is soiled and creased. He is pale and ill-looking. His face and hair are cleaner than hers giving the impression that she has been in the bed much longer than him. With the upstage wall on the ground the bed is now surrounded on three sides by plasterboard walls. There is a small window high on one of the side walls but the glass has been painted black. The bed is covered in a dirty floral duvet. When the wall falls the* DAUGHTER *looks out to the audience. She is completely lifeless.*

DAUGHTER. I'm in the bed. The panic has sucked me dry again 'til all that's left is ta start over. I get that tiredness turn to tight... and I give in ta the words. I let go. Go.

DAD *explodes and performs a story from his childhood.*

DAD. FUCK FUCK FUCK FUCK FUCK FUCK fucking hell fucking hell fuck fuck fuck Jesus fuck!! Fucking hell!! DAN DAN!! Me in the bed. I can feel these blankets like a big sea and me a little shrimp ways underneath!! Feel them wrapped around me bony body ribs making me stay in the bed. Squeeze me lungs out of me gob making me shout, 'Fucking hell get out of the bed, Maxie!! You're late!!' I swing me legs out of the bed already running I run inta tha jacks! There's me big brother Gerry on the jacks having an early-morning crap!! I smack him a left hook!! Shmack!! He hits the ground like the sack of shit he is!! 'I'll deal with you later, kiddo!' Splish splash run the tap and get scrubbing me face!!

DAD *and* DAUGHTER. Gotta be clean!! Havta look sharp!

DAD. Look in the mirror at the fifteen-year-old me looking back! 'Gotta get to work, Maxie! Only fourteen seconds to save the planet Earth, Flash!' Spin back to the bedroom and into the suit!! A bit damp from washing it last night but fuck it! Isn't it always damp from its late-night wash!? Have ta be clean! Gotta get going! Inta the wet shirt! On with the damp suit! Jesus I'm the smart one! Sharp is what I am!! Outta my smelly hole gaff, the stink of the hot sweet milk in the air, a breakfast puke! A family of lazy fucks huddled around the electric heater like laboratory rats, I leave the fucks behind. Shame shame!! Fucking shame!! I'm at the bus stop! Bus stops and I'm on! The usual faces stuck in their morning sleep! 'Great workers of Ireland! Is it not time to drag this priest-ridden, second-rate, potato-peopled country of ours into the twentieth century before we're spat into the next shagging hundred years?' They half-smile back like I'm a fucking psycho! Fuck 'em! I sit down in my usual spot!! Twitching twitching 'cause I gotta be there! Gotta be at work. Bus stops and I'm running. My damp suit tight around my legs like glue almost! I see the shop. Stop dead still and breathe it all in. Read the sign on the pearly gates. 'Robson's Furniture Emporium.' I'm fifteen and I'm working. But working in the storeroom!!

DAUGHTER. That fucking suit! Didn't I tell ya ta wear something scruffy, ya uppidy bollix!

DAD. I ignore the storeroom boss, Eugene, a great big ball of sweat with trousers hanging off his damp arse wanting to be free of it all. I stay silent and work! The furniture all wrapped up in plastics and paper, I get working!

DAUGHTER. Good lad!

DAD. Shifting the stock around like chess pieces. Vans pull up to the big corrugated door which snaps open! A great big hungry mouth and us the little storeroom hungry tongues gobbling up the furniture and packing them away!! But I'm the hungriest tongue of all 'cause I love the fucking work!!

DAUGHTER. He loves the fucking work!

DAD. Work work work work work work work work!!!
Satisfuckinfaction, boys, satisfuckinfaction! Fat Eugene
calls

DAUGHTER. Teabreak!

DAD. ... and out with the tabloids and teabags!! Fuck that!! I sit
alone! My damp suit steaming steam off it! Sit with me little
notebook marked 'Enemies' and jot down all the bad things
they throw in my direction!! Eugene's cavernous mouth
spewing out the funny talk.

DAUGHTER (*punchline*). Shiny knob!! I'll give ya a shiny
knob! (*Roars laughing, stops and growls*.) Ya Prince fucking
Charles.

DAD. Fat Eugene fucking hates me, boy. Wait 'til you're the
boss, Maxie-lad! By fuck there'll be some arses kicked then,
boys.

DAUGHTER. Right, lads!

DAD. And head down I work and work and work and work!!
And my body like some slick machine and my brain keen
and fast!! I rise up the stairs from the storeroom. I feel its
blackness on my back leave as I step onto the sales floor.
And all colour returns as the beautiful cabinets and couches
stretch out in front of me on the blue baise. I watch the
salesmen at their work. I look at their easy manner and stand
as they chat 'comfort' to the customers. Like royalty they
look or something. Their hands barely touching the fine
fabrics and polished tables as they waltz around the store to a
music inside their heads. I take out my other notebook
marked 'Salesman' and jot it all down. I watch the eyes of
the customers oohhhing and ahhing as the salesman lays
on the superlatives, spinning out the patter that crackles in
the air. I listen to the humour of the sales floor reeling in
the wallets, adding the VAT and tickling the tills. I watch the
teary eyes of the salesman as he waves a lost sale goodbye...
only to turn on his heels all hungry and smiling as he spies a
couple slouch inta a three-piece suite. I write the words,
'This will all be mine. One day', and I feel a horn battle
against my damp pants to be free. What a fucking beginning,

boy! By fuck, Cork, I'll lay ye out and fla the hole off ya!!
Oh yes!! Bring it on, boys. Bring it on! Is there no end to
me?! Is there no end to me, tell me?! For have I not arrived,
Dan Dan!! Have I not arrived, Dan Dan!! DAN DAN!! DAN
DAN!! DAN DAN!! DAN DAN!! DAN DAN!!

DAD *panics and falls to the bed. The* DAUGHTER *begins
to panic.*

DAUGHTER. He stops/it stops/his panic putting an end to him
and a start to me/I see that silence/oh Christ/fill it fast!/feel
it race towards me all full of the loneliness/think fast of of
of of of/my body!/my body ache is what I feel now/that fills
my head/that packs the silence with the smell of dust and
piss/but my body ache is.../my curvy back!/the walls are
still and silent with no thump pa de thump any more/they
just stand looking down on me and him/it was me and
she/but she is dead/I watch my mam die, ya know/get the
words in my head/they line up/I feel the words line up and
use my mouth like a cliff edge/they jump/fall fast with an
ugly-scream/my body ache/the smell of piss and shit/stunted
and twisted girl/mouth an angry hole/me the dust mite is
what I am/I can feel me sit in me and must know that this is
my body/but no control/mouth like a cliff edge/body a thick
duvet lump/smelling my body smell/all stale/give a little
puke then/watch the puke take to the duvet where once was
flowers but now all muck/all is muck and dust/he stops his
big talk and I see a silence that needs packing with words/oh
Christ/calm/'calm' is a small word ya can't shout/calm is
what I want/I ask my head for 'calm'/my head gets all
blocked with muck/must think fast then/try to think through
the muck inside my head/why did I think of muck?/mustn't
think of muck any more/must think of 'sky' so to open my
head and speak out lots of other words/the word 'sky'
breaks through the muck and gives me 'blue' and 'space'
and 'white clouds' and 'summers'/my head sets free on
images I can't talk of/too big they are/but it brings me some
little ease not to be speaking with words and just lying in
the picture of a blue sky dotted in clouds/not to be thinking
of the muck/not to be thinking of the bed/the fucking
bed/my life my life my life/think fast/the sky and clouds

fold inta the grey and pack inta a box marked 'muck'/fuck it!/so I try to think of my name/what is my name?/did she call me my name?/she called me Princess. I watched her die/I'm a child/no!/I'm a woman/I *was* a child/I was ten/I'm a woman/what is ten and ten?/could it be ten years?/ten years of me and her in the bed/what is the banging, Mam? I ask/the walls are getting closer?/what makes the walls getting closer? I ask/ it's a fairytale, she says/we are in a fairytale/we're waiting for a prince/wait for the prince, love/wait for his kiss/wait for his kiss/ten years and we wait for the prince/we get *him*/he calls himself Dad/says he's my dad/is he my dad? I ask the walls/but the walls don't answer 'cause the walls are dead and silent/the bastards/all full of the big talk is what he is/I remember my dad as a shadow and a voice/now I want for the shadow back/I face his ugly mush and showered with spit and tooth decay for a week now it seems/with his big talk/all full of the big talk/I get his story of furniture and then know he must be my dad/ 'furniture' my whole life up until the walls banging/the walls are getting closer/but I fill the silence and let him talk and I act out this Dan Dan and Sparkey and all the men/for what am I if I'm not words?/I'm empty space is what I am/what am I if I'm not words I'm empty space/so I learn the men and play them big/we fill the room with what he was until he stops/he stops/looks all afraid and tries to sleep/like it were some nightmare or something/and him just remembering this dream life of his/but a nightmare it seems/that story of Dublin/of dirty Dublin Dan Dan!/which gets me at the book/ (*She pulls out a worn filthy softback novella.*) this book that Mam did read and opened up a story of colour/a story outside of the bed/outside of the room/ outside in the outside/a story of romance/I watched my mam die so I must now read alone/can I read this story as she did?/my big question is can I read the story as Mam did? /and fear won't let me try/'cause maybe I can't/afraid to start to read/but I must/and I have to read as she did and find that place again, don't I?/to break free/to get free/to be free as she and me did/to be out/to be outside of this/to not have to think/but to allow a story of love to take me up/to set me free/of this/of him/of me.

DAD. SHUT THE FUCK UP!!

DAUGHTER. I CAN'T!

DAD. I'm trying to sleep!!

DAUGHTER. What's the point!! You should talk to me. Why don't we talk? Ya stopped talking to me!

DAD. I tried talking to ya, ya stumpy bitch!

DAUGHTER. Well, try again!

DAD. I want to sleep!

DAUGHTER. You won't be able to sleep.

DAD. I won't be able while we're talking, so shut the fuck up!

DAUGHTER. You won't be able when it's silent! You should face up to it! We're awake and that's the way it is in here!

DAD. I've got nothing to talk to you about.

DAUGHTER. We're talking now!

DAD. Yeah but about nothing!

DAUGHTER. It's filling the gaps, isn't it?!

DAD. It's making the gaps! If we didn't talk there would be no gaps! There'd be quiet! A great big field of quiet! That's what I want!

DAUGHTER. We can't have quiet!

DAD. Well, I could!

DAUGHTER. Don't!

DAD. I could! Talking is what *you* want! I want sleep! I'm not here for you, ya know! (*He goes to get out of the bed.*)

DAUGHTER. Don't go!

DAD. *I* can walk!

DAUGHTER. Don't!

DAD. I could!

DAUGHTER. Don't!

DAD. I could do what I want! My legs are in great shape!

DAUGHTER. Don't!

DAD. You fuck! You little bollix! It just crept up on me! Ya got me talking about something when talking to you is the fucking last thing on my mind! You've got the words bubbling up from inside me and making me spit out and talk, ya little puke! Now I've started I can't stop!

DAUGHTER. We both can't stop! That's all part of it!

DAD. 'It'? What the fuck is 'it'?

DAUGHTER (*giggling*). Me, you, the bed, time!

DAD. Both of us have stopped!

DAUGHTER. But not at the same time!!

DAD. I'll fucking stop! I'll rip me tongue out!

DAUGHTER. Ya wouldn't!

DAD. I could chew it off! I could tear me ears off me head and get some sleep! Find some rest! Let you do the talking!

DAUGHTER. Ya wouldn't do that!

DAD. The point is, I could! I could do it and then who would ya talk to? And what do you mean, I wouldn't? What makes you know what I would or wouldn't do, Dan Dan? I fucking will, ya cheeky cunt! (*He begins to chew his tongue. He screams.*) Yarrah fuck!!

DAUGHTER *laughs*.

You're making me leave!

DAUGHTER. Don't!

DAD. I can go! (*His mouth bleeds.*)

DAUGHTER. No, don't!

DAD. The point is I might! The point is I might go! The point is the point is… (*Slight pause.*) I'm bleeding!

DAUGHTER. What?

DAD (*devastated*). I'm alive. (*Pause.*) I'm still alive. Fuck.

DAUGHTER (*to herself, delighted*). I'm alive!

DAD (*shouts*). Back back back back back...

DAUGHTER (*overlapping*). Back back back back back back...
(*She laughs.*)

DAD (*overlapping*).... baCK BACK BACK BACK BACK
MAXIE!!! I stand in my damp tight suit, my fifteen-year-old
hands twitching twitching twitching, my eyes fixed calm on
Mr Bee. It seems only him stands between me and my
destiny. I watch his seventy-year-old baggy suit and hound-
dog eyes standing in the ke ke ke ke ke kitchen department
like some sad museum piece.

DAD. Give him a Maxie smile. Nice.

DAUGHTER. Ya know, Maxie, but ya ke ke ke ke keep that
suit looking lo lo lovely.

DAD. 'Ah thanks, Mr Bee. Are ya ready to head home then?'
We stand at the bus stop. And then in the bus and I listen to
the stories he patches together with the phrase,

DAUGHTER. And another fu funny thing...

DAD. I smile the smile of a friend. Truth is I hate the dusty
fucker. I hate his soft old ways, his tatty photo of his dead
wife Pa pa pa pa pa Peggy, those greaseproof-wrapped
sandwiches all sweaty and thick with butter, that morning
tradition he has of sitting in the shop ca ca ca ca ca canteen
smoking a lucky cigar before the shop door opens. I hate him
all. But I smile, though. I learn everything about him and
when I go home I jot it down in a notebook marked,

DAD *and* DAUGHTER. 'How to K K K K K Kill Mr B B B B
B Bee.'

DAD. He tells me he's lost his sense of smell. I draw a star
beside it and send myself to sleep whispering 'destiny' over
and over and over. Next day he answers his doorbell. 'All
right, Mr Bee, ready for the off then?!'

DAUGHTER. Good to see ya, Ma Maxie! Step in, son.

DAD. He waddles back into the kitchen. I follow. I run the tap for a glass of water but fill it with paraffin. I turn all clumsy and whoops-a-daisy, I spill the paraffin all over Mr Bee's jacket sleeves and lucky cigar which peeps out from his breast pocket like a shy little doggy. 'Just water!' I say to Mr Bee's odourly challanged no no no no no no nose.

DAUGHTER. Sure let it da dry, then!

DAD. We arrive at Robson's Furniture Emporium, me worn with his endless drivelling, him drenched in paraffin itching for his morning ci ci ci ci ci cigar. I watch as he places the cigar in his mouth and roots for his matches. Watch his cocktail-sausage fingers fumble the matchbox like it were a large snot. I turn and hear the click of the match off the box. I hear the tear of the strike. And I walk from the small canteen for the storeroom as Mr Bee explodes into 'fla fla flames' and lights my future upwards. (*Slight pause.*) He loved his butter, Mr Bee. By fuck he was burning for five hours, boy! And I mean, who would have believed it? (*Laughs.*) I'm a saleman. (*Screams.*) Dan Dan!! Dan Dan?? DAN DAN MY FUCK WIT VAN MAN!!

DAUGHTER. I'm here boss, I'm here!

DAD. For fuck sake, man!! Aren't these gone yet!

DAUGHTER. They're gone now! They're on the way!! They're in the van!!

DAD. They're fucking in front of me, Dan Dan!! What's the fucking point of me selling the shagging things if they're left here to gather dust!! It's not ours now so fucking get a move on!

DAUGHTER. We're working hard, boss!

DAD. Don't tell me what work is, Dan Dan!! Who the fuck are ye ta tell me that! You're only a snivelling lazy cunt with less sense than a stupid fucking donkey! You're a fucking stupid donkey-man, Dan Dan!!

DAUGHTER *makes the noise of a donkey.*

There's a science documentary in you, Mister Donkey-Man!!

DAUGHTER. You're a gas man, boss!

DAD. Where the fuck is Fat Eugene?

DAUGHTER. In the stores, boss!

DAD. Send the fat fucker up here!! I need something to punch!

DAUGHTER. Ya called, boss!!

DAD (*punches*). 'Schmack!!'

DAUGHTER. I'll clear him up will I, boss?

DAD. Tell him he's fired when he comes around. When I was fifteen, lads, that fat fuck stank my air real bad. Like working with a giant poo poo always hanging around.

DAUGHTER. Ah very funny, boss!

DAD. And Dan Dan!

DAUGHTER. Yes, boss.

DAD. You watch your back yerself or I'll tear lumps outta ya, boy!

DAUGHTER. Fair enough!!

DAD. 'Now move it!!' Twenty-three and Robson's Furniture Emporium dances to my beat. I keep a book marked 'Customers'. I know where they live. I visit their locals in the evenings. I call into the pub and... 'Jesus, Danny, how's tricks!! That wall unit working out fine, is it?! No I won't have a... ah give us a mineral so!'

DAD *and* DAUGHTER. Another pub another sale...

DAD. 'Seamus! How are ya?! Wa ya ya a halla a wha?!' I know everything about them. Before they know it they're chatting personals in the pub jacks, 'Ya'd wanta get that mole seen to, Robbie! By fuck that doesn't look healthy at all!!!' I fit in sixteen pubs a night! Now that's stamina! Sundays and I'm doing the rounds on the football pitches! Cheering for my customers, being their best friend. 'Great shot, Trevor!! Good man!!' I sit in bingo halls and chat recipes with the old ladies during the interval. I learn off the recipes and spout them out! What do I know about food and cookery?!

DAD *and* DAUGHTER. Couldn't give a bollix me!

DAD. But then I slip in, 'Jesus, ya should see the colourful worktops we've got, girls! Magic!!'

DAUGHTER. I'll pop in tomorrow so!

DAD. And it's all worthwhile. Robson's is my success! Mine alone! Twenty-three and Cork is mine! I'm loved by them! But the point is! I mean, the point is they're spending their cash in my shop!! (*Screams.*) Dan Dan!!

DAUGHTER. Yeah, boss!!

DAD. What's the problem, boy?!

DAUGHTER. We need an extra pair of hands, boss.

DAD. 'Get out of the fucking way so!' I take the three-seater in my arms like a newborn baby and sling it in the back of the van. Join the three van men by way of supervision. 'Who the fuck are you?'

DAUGHTER. Terry.

DAD. How long have you been with us, Gary?

DAUGHTER. Two years now!

DAD. Two years? Well, shift your hole for the boss. How are you then, Sparkey?

DAUGHTER. Tops, boss!!

DAD. Jesus, you're one ugly fucker! Married are ya?

DAUGHTER. Not yet, boss.

DAD. I wouldn't hold your breath, Sparkey boy! D'ya know sick people would pay good money to see a face like yours.

DAUGHTER. Ah yer a gas man, boss!

DAD. 'Drive on, Dan Dan!!' And off we go. I feel the tension hang in the air. I stare ahead sensing their grubby hands pumping out the sweat. Just waiting for my roars. They hate me. Do I give a fuck? Do I bollix!

DAUGHTER. That's Mrs Dexter's there, boss!!

DAD. 'Well, get a fucking move on.' I stand on the kerb surveying the three stooges grapple with the wall unit like it were made out of clitoris. 'Get your back into it, Sparkey.' We enter Mrs Dexter's gate and up through her garden as pristeen as anything ya'd see on the telly. Fine roses them. Fancy-floral. Lovely. 'Mrs Dexter, Eileen! We've arrived! Early as usual! Step aside, love, and we'll get the job done.'

DAUGHTER. Ya'll have a cup a tea, will ya?!

DAD. A cup of tea! Ah now don't be spoiling these fellas! Sure they don't even know what tea is!!

DAUGHTER. Very funny, boss!!

DAD. No fucking mistakes now.

DAUGHTER. All right, lads! Easy now, Sparkey!

DAD. I imagine the pressure on Dan Dan's tiny brain as he leads the wall unit between the straights of Mrs Dexter's doorway. His light-blue eyes unblinking begin to seep sweat and glisten from his grubby little face. I watch his thick fingers like... like chicken drumsticks bend around the wall unit. The veins on his head balloon with thick cholesterol and my voice. His back, the size of a horse's, inches further and further into the house. For a second, probably less, I feel what amounts to a tiny pride as Dan Dan and his idiot helpers place the wall unit against Mrs Dexter's sitting room wall. Oh, very good. Very very good. (*Screams.*) 'TAKE YOUR FUCKING TIME, WHY DON'T YA!' (*Calmly to audience.*) No matter how often you remind someone that you're the boss... it can never be enough, believe me, boy. (*Screams.*) 'Ah for fuck sake, Dan Dan, YA FUCKING RETARD!!'

DAUGHTER. What is it, boss?

DAD *begins to panic a bit and covers himself with a blanket. The* DAUGHTER *is immediately nervous.*

Is that all we're doing then? Daddy? Dad?

The silence closes in on the DAUGHTER *and she begins to panic. She looks at the book and braces herself to read it. She begins to read but is beginning to lose it as the words spin out of control.*

Katie was small with delicate bones and an air of vulnerability that drew men to her like bees to honey. Across the massive ballroom the light from the chandelier speckled down on debutantes as they cavorted with one another. Handsometall mentheir long backs and angular jawlines seemed dull and dreadfully vain to Katie otheryoungwomen with wanton eyes and... oh Christ... and and poutinglipspositionedthem-selvesaroundthevasthall, like dead mannequins, Katie thought. For fuck sake calm calm calm calm... for although angelic-andsereneinappearanceKatie'smindhousedawickedwit... oh fuck/I know it so well!/each word I know is stuck in her voice/ a voice I can't speak/I feel my head panic and reach out to get to the next sentence/I feel that sentence fall away from me/I see the calm face of my mam/she reads the book and the words not fire but pass with a music from her voice/my voice so ugly/but must keep talking to fill this fucking silence!/is this it?/already I'm living some manky future with him of the big talk and me of the fast/me scuttering words like a sick arse/him crashing the words about/bruising the air!/ohh fuck this/fill it fill it fill it fill it FILL IT/think of Katie/(*Blocks her eyes.*) look through the grey and think of Katie in the book/her skin!/I see her skin!/ 'delicate' is what they say/'ivory' is how they say it/and on a horse/her hair 'whipped by the wind' as she goes faster and faster/and the landscape 'lush' and pastoral/try to place me there I make the lush all damp and old dust/fuck/fill it fill it/forget me to be her/and Katie in her room/all big as she watches the light on her face as she hears his voice from the study below/and lipstick/and something in her eye/some 'cunning'/and her mother/Katie's mother/so beautiful she is/she calls/he's waiting in the study/she calls with a 'cheeky' voice/ and there's laughter in my mam's voice as she reads/and I can see Katie smile/good fuck/my fucking life/I can see her stand and walk/her lightness/the sun leaving her back as she faces her future with him/her future/while mine is all deadened/ all twisted/all sad/all fucking bad/I can't feel the book, Mam!/Jesus holy fuck!

DAD *sits up and watches her screaming, crying. He shows no sympathy for her. He looks like he may even laugh.*

What did ya do to Mam?

He doesn't answer.

Are you really my dad?

DAD *breathes in deep and takes off once more.*

DAD (*screaming triumphant*). EUROPE DAN DAN!!

DAUGHTER (*overlapping*). Answer it!

DAD (*overlapping*). Hotel dining room, furniture delegates breakfasting on muesli and fucking yogurt! 'Jeez, I'd murder a sausage sangwidge' but steer my energies towards progress! I'm sharp! A new suit marks me out from the rest!

DAUGHTER (*screams*). Answer it!!

DAD. 'Good morning, gentleman!! Bon jour as they say!!' Before I know it I'm chomping through a thing called a croissant, swigging a black coffee and acting more Continental than Sacha Distel! 'You've gotta be ahead a the pack to try patent shoes but you know, Richard, my English friend, I've got two words for you "Dirk" "Bogart". Granted he was a steamer but what a dresser!!' Talking to some Norwegian bloke called Lars I hear his new line in wardrobes and dining-room tables are A-one! 'Well, that sounds like I might be interesting in that, Lars!!' Trouble is everyone fucking knows! 'Sorry, Richard! Can I have a word in your ear, Lars?' Out with the francs and me and my buddy Lars kicking our way through a Paris Springtime! Into some classy strip place and Lars sucking at the end of a bottle of champagne. He fucking loves me, boy! 'I can tell that yer a right little goer, hey Larsie?!' I call over two slappers and slip them a few hundred! Before I know it me and Lars and the two slappers are rolling around a giant bed with the hungriest genitals in Gay Paree! Suddenly it stops! Lars tells the girls to fuck off and then faces me! In perfect English he asks me to bend over, that he wants to lick my arse. I face the pillow and feel the wet tongue tickle my crack... reminding me that the last time I took a shit it was courtesy of British Airways. He then assumes the position and asks for a good licking himself. I face his hairy hole and what stares back at me... what stares back at me are the faces of my competitors rapt in jealousy. (*He licks.*) The deal is mine, Dan Dan.

DAUGHTER. You're a marvel, boss.

DAD. You better believe it, boy. Now get those fucking wasters Terry and Sparkey to unload the new merchandise.

The DAUGHTER*'s playing of the characters is tougher now. Like she's pushing him.*

DAUGHTER. My wife thinks the world of you, boss.

DAD. She's a wise woman. In some respects.

DAUGHTER. Ever think of getting a wife yourself?

DAD. A wife? And what the fuck would I be needing with a wife?

DAUGHTER. To do the cooking, boss.

DAD. And by fuck but Dan Dan was making some sense! Recalling a young quiet thing who clung to her mam in the bingo hall, I make my moves. I spot her reading some romantic tacky book. Clear my throat to be heard above the bingo scribbling, my first words are, 'You should marry me, you know.'

DAUGHTER. Congratulations, boss!

DAD. 'Why thanks very much, Dan Dan!' I enroll her in an evening class entitled 'Create Your Own Dinner Parties'. Each month the house packed with vol-au-vents and fields upon fields of cocktail sausages. Pastry clogging her hands like sticky winter mittens, for fuck sake!! Mister and misses me and her. Her done up like a porcelain doll, me like a life-sized Action Man! What a team! I invites my best customers! They fucking love me!

DAUGHTER. Jesus, Maxie, but this is a great spread!

DAD. You should see the new Norweeeegen range in the bedding department, Bernard! Such bargains!

DAUGHTER. My God, but you've transformed the city!

DAD. And he's right! I've done it all. It's all my doing. Take another cheesy vol-au-vent, Bernard, plenty more from where that came from, boy!' (*He laughs. Pause. Tone turns grave*.) Then I spy 'him'. A new face. A face all tanned and handsome. A suit of light grey and loose. A laugh of a rich man. He walks towards me his eyes slowly smiling then. His long hand closing around my squatty fingers.

DAUGHTER. I'm a friend of Bernard's. Marcus Enright.

DAD. I feel the name etch its way through my head and sit behind the back of my eyes and know already that I will never be free of that name. Marcus Enright. An ex-barrister, he tells me he's going to open a furniture shop in Dublin. How his two sons share his interest in

DAUGHTER. Quality furniture.

DAD. I fucking hate him. I want to open his face with the corkscrew I carry around. Want to drag him on to our new patio and barbecue the posh bollix. He's making me feel cheap. I watch him flinch as he lowers the Blue Nun from his mouth. I vow to see his business fucked. I promise to gobble him up and shit him out. Fuck it, I need an ally, though!

DAUGHTER (*her own voice*). Ya need a son!

DAD. I go at the wife all doggy-style. Grabbing her round arse in my prawn-cocktail-stained hands with the dinner party and no doubt Marcus fucking Enright in full swing down below. It's my first ever fuck. Never had the time, interest, want before until now. My tiny prick grapples to make its mark. Like sky diving into a giant sky called 'fanny', like throwing a ball up Patrick's Street, like getting up on the Shannon Estuary, I jiggle about for all of two minutes before I shoot my load. 'Never doubt the potency of my sperm, woman!' Nine months later and it's all push push pushing! 'Til out it drops! Not a son at all but a girl!

DAUGHTER. Hello, Dad!

DAD. Fuck! Undaunted I get her reading baby books on her first goo gaa! Books about furniture! Pop-up books about chairs and tables. Her first word,

DAUGHTER. Stool.

DAD. 'Ah that's excellent, sweetie!' Her first drawing,

DAUGHTER (*like a baby*). A chest of drawers.

DAD. Dan Dan, my daughter!

DAUGHTER. She's beautiful, boss!

DAD. She's a fucking genius, man, don't mind that beauty stuff. Looks fade, boy! She takes after her old man. Time for a new sign on the old shop, Dan Dan. Fuck that Robson's Furniture Emporium bollix. From now on it's Maxwell Darcy and Daughter.

DAUGHTER. Maxwell Darcy and Daughter?

DAD. Happy days, Dan Dan. Happy days!

DAUGHTER (*her own voice, hard*). I don't remember them, Dad.

DAD *begins to panic.*

I'll speak the only thing that's clear to me just ta shut you out. I remember I fire meself out of this bed and sling my ten-year-old bikini on.

DAD *tries to hide under the blanket. She continues with conviction.*

It's all yellow with pink dots and I fasten it around my chest… as if I had anything to hide. I've got awful problems fastening the bikini but then feel the long fingers of Mam click me into shape and pat me on the head. I smell the hand cream on her fingers. I look at her fingers made rough from all the pastry. All those millions of vol-au-vents turning her hands to cake. All for you and that fucking shop. I tell her that she's beautiful because to me she is. As usual she stays quiet and we get the bus to the beach with the summer heat sending the bus shimmering towards our stop. 'Might Dad one day blow up, Mam?' I think that was the question I

asked. And she started to laugh. The people on the bus
turned and smiled because her laugh was so loud and happy.
I had a good old laugh meself thinking of you blowing up in
our new fitted kitchen all over the Formica worktops. In my
laugh I let a fart which made Mam laugh even louder. All
laughed out we lay in the water as the tide tippled up over
us and both looking up towards the sun. Scrunched-up
faces. I turned over and lay on Mam and kissed the salt off
her face. The dry sea salt on her beautiful face like she were
a frosted bun I told her. And then she hugged me so hard it
almost squeezed the air out of my inflatable-swan ring. That
was nice. And that's when I went for a walk. I left Mam
lying on the beach. That would be the last time I would see
her as a healthy girl. I walked over the dunes spying on the
teenagers snatching at their crotches. I talked to a priest
sunbathing with the Bible and his crippled mother who
sucked on oranges like they were going out of fashion. He
read the story about Jesus in the desert to me and squatted a
wasp with the Gospel of St John. Squished it dead. I walked
on pretending that I was Jesus in search of water with only
hours to live. I pretended I was a desert rabbit and ran
through the sharp rushes like a right mad yoke. The rushes
like nasty pins and needles firing me faster and faster and
faster and faster. The soft sand sent spitting from my heels.
My skinny arms and legs a mad blur. My springy hair
springing out straight from my speed. My head free. Free of
you and that fucking furniture talk. And then I felt no
ground underneath me. Like the dog in the Roadrunner
cartoons I tried running in the air. It was sort of funny until I
fell down. And I fell down into this big hole. And right up to
my waist I was covered in shit. I soon stopped trying to
catch any clean air and just breathed in the shit air. I had a
little puke. Puked up the cola bottles I ate on the bus. I
wiped my mouth of the puke with a hand covered in shit. I
spat the shit out and started to climb up a little ladder out of
the concrete hole. And I didn't even cry. And that's the story
of the day I got the polio. From then on everything went
mad, didn't it? And ya know a day doesn't go past where I
think I should have stayed in that place. How fucking happy
I'd be.

DAD *is speechless. It is clear that he has been touched by the beauty of her story.*

Why is it that's a clear picture and nothing else is? Do you have any answers for me, Dad?

DAD. I don't know what anything is. Everything's all fucked up.

DAUGHTER. Then speak of Dublin then, Dad! Speak of Dublin but don't get all afraid like before and just speak up until right this moment, Dad… right this moment for me. Just let go and say it as it was! Let go, Maxie! Let go! Let go! (*Overlapping.*) GO GO GO GO GO GO GO GO GO GO GO GO!!!!

Using her energy he throws himself into his days in Dublin.

DAD (*overlapping*). 'Fuck fuck fuck fuck fuck fuck fuck fucking hell fucking hell fuck fuck fuck Jesus fuck!! Fucking hell!! Dan Dan!!' DUBLIN!! DIRTY DUBLIN!

DAUGHTER (*as herself*). Jesus, Maxie, I can't see it working! The shops in rag order!

DAD (*under serious pressure*). I'll be the judge of that! Am I not the boss?! Is this not the boss stuck right in front of ya, ya fucking Dublin cunt!?

DAUGHTER. It's too expensive for our clientele! We haven't a chance to shift it, Maxie!

DAD. 'Listen to me, ya little college shite! The fact a the matter is… the fact a the matter is… I mean the fact a the matter is… arrah fuck Schmackkk! Brian pick him up and fuck him out! Get yer backs into it, lads! This is history! What man has opened three furniture shops on the same day throughout Dublin!? What man? Answer me that, Marcus Enright? Answer me that, you of the tight hole!! No fucking, man! No fucking Jackeen, either, lads! Sure doesn't it take a Cork man to build! God himself was from Glasheen! He fucking well was, boys! Knew him well! By Christ, God was a worker!! Work work work! Continents were born! Work a bit harder the seas were flowing!

Scratched his arse and out popped Britain! By fuck I have ya Dublin! Ya arrogant little pup! Eleven o'clock and these doors swing open, Brian! Swing open!' I leave the shop! The muscles on me neck showing off those pumping veins like a thick cock! I turn and read the sign! 'Maxie's Furniture Super Shop'! A flash of you pictures in me head with your twisted body soaked in the polio! SHIT!! SHIT!! I walk! I walk through Dublin! I feel the power in my body! I could have driven but walking is more powerful, isn't it? Walking is where it's at, boys!! Like a great big battleship I walk the length of O'Connell Street towering over the Dublin scum. 'Jesus, yer not so uppidy now, are ya?! Not now that Maxie's in town! Three shops in one day! A fucking record, man!' I swing onto Parnell Street with the power of a planet, the grace of a movie star, the Michael Collins of the furniture world! And there!! And there are the cameras!! Photographers piled up outside Maxie's Furniture Super Shop Number Two! Waiting! Waiting for the one and only! Waiting for the man himself!!

Cameras flashing.

Jesus, thanks for coming, lads!

DAUGHTER. Congratulations, Maxie.

DAD. 'Thanks, son, thanks!'

DAUGHTER. Fantastic shop, Maxie!

DAD. 'That's very kind of ya! She's a beauty all right! She's a cracker!'

DAUGHTER. I believe there's problems with the Moore Street shop, Maxie! People are saying ya won't make your deadline of eleven o'clock! Do you want to comment on that?

DAD. 'Sure that's a nonsense! That's just people talk! Are people talking about that? Ya know the way that people love the talk? Well, that's all that is! That's people talking! Talking their mouths off! That's all it is! She'll be open at eleven all right, boys! As sure as Sophia Loren has legs and Marcus Enright's a prick that shop will be open!' They laugh their journalistic laughs and lap me all down on their tiny little pads. I make them me friends, in one smile taking them all in. 'Now ya can follow me if ya like, lads, but I'm off to Marlbora Street to see the next shop swing open its doors on the delights of bedding, the practicalities of Formica, the elegance of brushed Dralon and the honesty of pine! Onward!' I march away! Their rain-macs rustling as they try to keep up with my pace!

DAD *and* DAUGHTER. Tickatocktickatocktickatocktickatock! Eleven o'clock eleven o'clock eleven o'clock eleven o'clock eleven o'clock eleven o'clock...

DAD. ... spins about me brainbox! Spins around like a bad friend, a scary ghost, a fucking devil of a time that is eleven o'clock! Another corner rounded and there she is! 'Gentlemen, Maxie's Furniture Super Shop Number Three.'

Cameras flashing.

'Jesus, but what a beautiful sight she is, lads, there with her Pearly Gates open! (*Getting emotional.*) And when I think of the little boy who used wash his one suit... one fucking suit, mind you, each night to be clean in the morning... ready for the work in the storeroom! Jesus, lads, when I think of the thousands of cabinets and wardrobes and three-piece suites at reasonable prices that have passed through my life! When I think of the friends I have made... the van men who've become family to me... D'you know, lads, but I have a charmed life! Like... like a fairyfuckingtale, lads. A fairyfuckingtale. Now onwards to Moore Street and eleven o'clock!' By fuck that was a performance worthy of honour! I didn't know I had it in me to be emotional! Isn't life a box of surprises all the same?! The walk feeling less powerful all of a sudden, though, as I belt up Henry Street with the paparazzi on tow! I feel the nerves twitching behind my eyes sending lumps into my throat like shite blocking drains! Good fuck! I turn onto Moore Street with all the grace of a milk cart with eleven o'clock ticking into time and...! (*He pauses and stares ahead, his face collapsing into failure, he whispers.*) Oh fuck. Oh Jesus. (*He suddenly screams.*) 'BRIAN!! BRIAN YA LITTLE FUCKER!! Is it not eleven o'clock and the doors still shut?!'

DAUGHTER. We're all over the place, boss!

DAD. 'Shut it! SHUT IT!! Shut your hole!!' I grabs hold of his hair and run! What's got into me?! I run through the shop smashing his head from wardrobe to table from cabinet to wall unit! I feel hair coming off in my fingers so I grab tighter! SCHLAPP!!! I take him to the office and open the door with his fucking head! SCHMAAAK! 'Ya little fucker! Make a fool a me will ya! We'll all have a laugh at Maxie, is that it!! Shmack! Schmack schmack! SCHMACK! SCHMACK! YA FAT BOLLIX!! YA FUCK! YA FUCK!' (*He stops. Cameras start to flash.*) Flash flash flash flash FLASH!! I leave! I leave it all behind and leave! And leave Dublin! FLASH!! I see my newspaper picture bent over Brian and smashing his head ta mush! Fuck Dublin! Leave and drive! My last image a giant furniture shop with Marcus Enright and Sons gilded in gold! Fuck him! Fuck it! Fuck Dublin! FUCK!!

Last camera flashes loudly.

A pause. Can he continue?

DAUGHTER. And then what, Daddy?

DAD. And then I return to Cork and see the wife and see you… I see *you*. (*Hard.*) And I see yer fucked-up body! I see how the polio has sent things wrong in *my* life! And I look at the wife who did this! What put it in my mind I can't say but I'm at the hardware shop and return to the house and I start building walls inside the house! Partition walls, ya know! And I make the space tight tight around you and yer mam! WHAT SHAME YOU GAVE ME! And I spend the nights building the walls so it's tight tight tight and getting tighter! And during the day it's… Dan Dan!! '*Great to have ya back, boss! Dublin was a bollix, I believe!*' Yerrah fuck, Dublin! '*Yer right, boss!*' We'll get back to old times, Dan Dan! That will be great, hah? And we work our arses off! By fuck we're shifting stock around Cork like we were Santa Clauses! '*How's the daughter, Maxie!*' 'Sure my daughter's dead, Dan Dan! She died when I was up in Dublin! The Dublin cunts!' I get home in the evening with a car full of

plasterboard and start at the walls! Thump pa thump pa
thump pa thump pa thump pa thump!! Your space getting
tighter and tighter! I feed ya bits of lunches I've robbed off
Dan Dan! For a while I think of killing ya straight off! But
this seems the better option! Of course it does!! Keep ya
alive I can think of what to do next! Nothing like a busy
head! Nothing like options! Sure that's business! Business is
all about options! Keep your options open and ya have
choice! 'AND CHOICE IS LIFE! Isn't that right, Dan Dan?'
'*Right as rain, boss!*' Thump pa thump pa thump pa thump
pa thump pa thump!! So I build more and more and more
walls! And one day a great big wall I build right around this
bed with you and yer mam in! Tight tight tight! Like a
lunchbox with two humans at home inside! It's perfect or
something! 'A good year isn't it, Dan Dan?!' 'A good year
isn't it, Dan Dan?' 'Another good year isn't it, Dan Dan!?'
Ten years of good years, Dan Dan! Ten years and the
nightmare of Dublin has fucked off to someone else entirely!
Ten years of feeding wife and daughter with Dan Dan's
lunches! Ten years and the people of Cork City FUCKING
GENUFLECT in FRONT OF ME! Now this! This is a life!
Dan Dan! DAN DAN!! (*More difficult now.*) You've got me
on the van with ya today! I read the pink docket and the
name of Mrs Dexter! A new wall unit for the old bitch. 'No
fucking mistakes now.' (*All fearful.*) I grab holda my end of
the wall unit and Dan Dan has his, backing his way into Mrs
Dexter's garden with her lovely red roses. Look at the
concentration swell Dan Dan's brain. Little dribbles of sweat
spit up on his fringe and edge their way down his face. My
head thumpathumpathumpa thumpa thumpa! 'Easy, Dan
Dan! Watch it, boy!' The strain showing on Dan Dan's body
the wall unit begins a nervous shake. I look and stare into
Dan Dan's eyes. And there… there in Mrs Dexter's
garden… there with all my customers peeping out through
the curtains at the new wall unit… there the nervous shake
turns into a wobble and I see the long fingers of Marcus
Enright tipple… tipple… tipple… tipple… (*Long pause,
then very controlled.*) Next thing ya know my red face
stands in the back of the van with Dan Dan lifting bits of
wall unit towards me. Him crying like a baby. 'Step up here,

Dan Dan.' And he does. '*I'm sorry, Maxie*.' And I give him a smile as he turns away and bends down to shift the broken wood. And my thumb flicks the Stanley blade 'til all that's left is to slit Dan Dan's throat! And I do. And I hold his head as my brainbox finally explodes to the trickle of Dan Dan's blood doing their own little funny race down his chest.

DAUGHTER. JESUS FUCK!! I get that tight tight tight in the belly holding on to all the hate I have for you! I want to bite and rip your fucking head off for that story you just blurted out like a casual fart! Why? Jesus, why the walls, you twisted sad shit of a man! I remember only the house getting smaller! I remember Mam whispering how we were in a fairytale and how with a kiss one day the house would open up! And open up back into space! And all the hammering all through the night! Thump pa thump pa thump pa thump pa thump pa thump!! Every night being pushed further and further into the tight until both of us in the bed and the hammering stops! AND THAT WAS YOU??! FUCKING HELL!! Can shame sour so much? Was it shame that turned to hate? It must have been hate! And we hold onto the book! And she reads it and when she does she can find love in her voice! And we stay awake… me and her. And I can't sleep so she talks and talks! Sometimes not making sense but sometimes making pictures with her words and words become my life as I try to fill the space, for what pictures do I really have but the four fucking walls that you've given me, you fucker! And my head like a great big lung at times so tight it could burst and other times let loose on landscapes! Let free! And you hear me read and forget the voice of my mam and read fast… killing the romance and making the landscapes so tight that they burst into tears!! My life is a fucking rant and not the story I wish it to be! I talk so fast so fast it's fucking killing the book and killing me! And all from you from you from you from you!

He watches her for a bit and then calmly finishes his story.

DAD. I enter the house and into the maze of the partitions. I've got the blood of Dan Dan on me hands. I make my way through the maze of the plaster walls and see you crying on the bed. I see Mam lying all hollow and dead like a doll.

When I lift her up you look at me. You don't know who
I am. And I take your mam's body out. I walk through the
maze with your crying fainter and fainter and the real world
mixing up to louder and asking me out of the house. Your
crying and the busy outside. And I stop. (*Pause.*) I stop and
listen and what I hear is silence then. (*Long pause.*) And it's
the first time in my life I've got room for silence. I stand
with the tiny body of your mam and let the silence clean me
out for a bit. (*Pause.*) And then... and then it starts as a tiny
thing in my mouth. I swallow it and it fills my stomach. And
then my brain gets hold of it and it fills my everything. I
have fear. It's fear. I'm afraid of my life outside. And I place
your mam on the ground and turn back until I arrive back at
the bed. And I get into the bed and face you as I do now.
And this is me talking. This is really me talking now. And I
don't have words for you. I don't have the right words for
you, love. I just want to sleep and get back to the silence but
I can't.

He is overcome. The DAUGHTER *hands her* DAD *the book.*
He begins to read it. He reads slow. She calms and listens.

'A hush came over the vast ballroom as Katie stood at the
top of the stairs. Her silken blonde hair brushed gently off
her bare shoulders as she made her descent. From the crowd,
whispers passed from gentleman to lady. She was beautiful.
Katie then walked through the crowd towards the man she
had seen at church. Turning to her his heart began pounding.
Could this be the same little girl who cycled so wildly
around the village? She took his hand in hers. The man was
shocked, and yet what could he do? Katie could feel the hard
gaze of the audience watching her impertinence. She allowed
it wash over her as she leaned towards him offering him her
kiss. And when they kissed, everything that had gone before
had been forgotten and everything in front of them was...
was joy.'

DAD *closes the book and looks at his* DAUGHTER.

Slowly the DAUGHTER *leans to her* DAD. *She kisses him*
softly on the forehead. He then kisses her. They sit back and
look at each other. She listens to the silence for a bit.

DAUGHTER. I'm in the bed. The panic is gone and all that's left is ta start over. I get that tiredness turn to calm... and I give in to sleep. I let go. Go.

The wall, which had crashed down, raises up and boxes them in once more as the lights fade off them.

Blackout.

The End.

HOW THESE DESPERATE MEN TALK

How These Desperate Men Talk was first performed (with the title *Fraternity*) at the Schauspielhaus Zürich on 18 December 2004. The cast was as follows:

DAVE   Matthias Schuppli
JOHN   Daniel Lommatzsch

Director   Erich Sidler
Designer   Karoline Weber
Lighting Designer   Jeannette Seiler
Dramaturg   Erik Altorfer

Characters

DAVE

JOHN

Lights fade up slowly.

A bare stage but for two middle-aged men of similar appearance sitting opposite each other. Their names are JOHN *and* DAVE, *and they are men from suburbia. Between them is a small square table.*

JOHN *holds a pistol to* DAVE's *face. We can't hear what they're saying below the static but it is clear that they're having a heated discussion.* DAVE *is seen to back down, the argument seemingly lost to the man with the gun.*

DAVE *and* JOHN's *general demeanour is on edge.*

This all lasts forty-five seconds. The static thankfully stops.

DAVE. It seemed right that it would be the anniversary. Seemed almost too perfect that today would have to be the day. Would have to be the same day a year on from the time you first saw her. How ordered it all was.

JOHN. How simple and true and right.

DAVE. How simple and true and right. Like the very first time you saw her in the park drinking her drink… like you gave life to her somehow.

JOHN. Like she just existed from that moment on.

DAVE. Right. You imagined her and there she was, taking her drink on the park bench that evening like she always did. Looking at the little quack-quacks neither interested nor disinterested. Just blank-looking. She looked blank to you and just then you realised that this is what attracted you to her. Her blankness.

JOHN. That's right.

DAVE. And as you followed her home that night from the park and followed her the next morning and afternoon you started giving her different personalities the same way you did to the hundreds of blank people you had followed about town. And in certain angles, certain lights, she became different people from your past. Your distant past. And by the end of the first week and after following her in and out of the shops and the parks and on and off buses... and as you looked at her sitting on the park bench and taking her drink and looking blankly at those little quack-quacks... you decided there and then who she was to you, John. You decided you were looking at your...?

DAVE *stops and waits*. JOHN *responds:*

JOHN. My mother.

DAVE. Your mother!? Haven't we done that before?

JOHN. Well, I don't know!

DAVE. I'm sure we have used your mother...

JOHN. Really?

DAVE. A little time ago.

JOHN. Are you certain?

DAVE. Certain? No, I'm not certain.

JOHN. Then just use it! USE IT! CARRY ON!

DAVE. Your much younger *mother* before you were born. Before she married your father? The young woman you had followed that first week and was following every week since... she meant this to you.

JOHN. Right.

DAVE. She may be going about her own life but what was important was that she was your mother to you. Simple. So as you showered that morning and walked around your flat, unconnected images and stories all featuring your mother and father seemed to follow you about. Traces of them started to stink up one room making you walk to another room.

JOHN. Nice image.

DAVE. Thanks.

JOHN. As a little…

DAVE. As a little boy you'd be up early. Woken with a sick stomach and sat at the kitchen table facing the soggy cornflakes with your father droning on about work. Like a boy would care! Like a six-year-old boy would take interest in insurance!

JOHN. I hated that insurance talk and 'cause that's all that my father spoke…

DAVE. You hated your father.

JOHN. Hated his fucking guts, Dave!

DAVE. You imagined him at work, how snivelling and pathetic he'd be. Smelling of Mother's soap, with his Tubberware lunches and how his work colleagues must have hated him!

JOHN. They did!

DAVE. What a sorry sight of a man he was! Christ! But as much as you hated your father it was your mother you hated more.

JOHN. But *why*?

DAVE. You'd use the morning to investigate this question. Today being the day it was… it was important to remind yourself of all the reasons. If you were going to do what you were going to do… you would have to be certain and revisit those terrible moments from when you were a little boy for this one last time.

JOHN. This is very good.

DAVE. Yeah?

JOHN. I'm enjoying this.

DAVE. Really?

JOHN. All this mother stuff, I like it.

DAVE. Yeah, but you liked the priest one too.

JOHN. The priest version was good but this has more truth about it.

DAVE. Really? You think this might be the truth?

JOHN. Well, that doesn't matter, does it?

DAVE. Doesn't it?

JOHN. The *exact* truth hardly matters, Dave. Are you joking!

DAVE. Of course, sorry. Then we're searching for what exactly?

JOHN. Difficult to say. We are definitely searching, though!

DAVE. We certainly are! No chance of a rest?

JOHN *clicks the trigger on the gun.* DAVE *quickly continues.*

You took in some fresh air in the outside so as to clear your head and spell out all these terrible moments in clear embarrassing details.

JOHN. Good.

DAVE. As a little boy in your house your mother would follow you about in her underwear. The only friend you ever brought home and she's in her bra and knickers while you're playing tiddlywinks in the kitchen. You're watching your friend's face as she presses her crotch against his arm. You scream and she pulls down your trousers and smacks your bare backside with a coat hanger. She makes your friend watch this and later on over hot milk and biscuits she calls your friend her 'prince'.

JOHN. The bitch!

DAVE. It's the day of your tenth birthday but you're at a neighbour's cocktail party and dressed like a miniature man in a black tuxedo and your mother's flirting with you and saying to the others,

JOHN. 'I've got rid of the husband for the night and here's my date! Isn't John handsome? Isn't he a hunk?'

DAVE. After about fifteen minutes of this you hide away beneath the stairs with a plateful of sausage rolls and a glass of fizzy lemonade. You sit in the darkness and sing 'Happy Birthday' to yourself 'til you're hauled out by a man, your mother grabbing you by the neck and placed in the middle of the room and telling you to sing *that* song.

JOHN. 'Sing that song you sing. The song about the elephant! Sing it, sing it, sing it, sing it, sing it, sing it, sing it!' She gets the adults to clap me on as my sausage-roll-belly begins to mix with all that fizz. It mixes bad! I'm on my hands and knees and being sick on the neighbour's rug. Fuck him! Another time and I'm in a supermarket with her. My teenage body jammed into a pair of tennis shorts and she's got me by the fish fingers and slapping my legs.

DAVE. 'I told you they were here! I told you the fingers were opposite the peas.'

JOHN. Another time and I'm sat on the large tricycle my bitch-mother bought me for my *fifteenth* birthday. I'm watching boys and girls ride their racing bikes while I'm made cycle up the centre of the road with my mother driving behind in her car… mother blaring the horn for all to see.

DAVE. Your mother was this type of woman, John. Your mind was settled and for the afternoon you focused again on the young woman you were following this past year. The young woman who had come to represent your mother to you. Knowing her daily routine you knew that she'd be in the library about now.

JOHN. She'd be there with her books and planning out her week.

DAVE. You felt no pangs of guilt,

JOHN. No!

DAVE. no worry,

JOHN. Never!

DAVE. no fear as you imagined that library seat empty this time tomorrow. You'd never spoken to the young woman before but that evening you'd hear her voice. That evening, just as you planned it, you'd talk about the lake and the ducks and the wonderful simple life of the duck. You would hear her voice until you finally decided not to hear her voice any more. To stop her voice and keep it forever stuck in the simple words of ducks.

JOHN lowers the gun and covers his eyes with both hands and continues carefully. DAVE *watches.*

JOHN. Already in my mind I have returned home from the park, Dave. I'm inside my flat and neither tense nor calm, Dave. I move about with a glass of wine, feeling the carpet on the soles of my feet, Dave. I ignore the little grass stains on my trousers, the slight tear on my shirt sleeves and feel pleased that no blood has marked me. And it's like I'm reborn somehow... or perhaps... yet born. In doing what I did I've erased the images of my mother from my past. Those wicked stories I've dragged around all these years. My mother both ceases to exist or ever exist. In the morning I will wake up and start a new life, Dave. In the morning the ducks will find the young woman's dead body in the bushes... and now it will be their time to look blankly at her.

A pause. JOHN *opens his eyes.*

DAVE. Well?

A pause. JOHN *looks at his shaking hands. They're covered in dried blood.*

Then:

JOHN. We'll go again!

DAVE. Oh Christ!

JOHN. From the start, come on!

DAVE. Again!?

JOHN. You heard!

DAVE. With what, though?

JOHN. What do you mean, 'With what?'?

DAVE. You want me to start over with anything different from before?

JOHN. You mean the details?

DAVE. Well, should I change them?

JOHN. The details are fine. Mother's not right. It *was* good but completely wrong.

DAVE. Are we getting any closer to who it is we're blaming?

JOHN. We must be. We've been doing this for quite a long time now. We must be closer.

DAVE. Unless we're repeating ourselves.

JOHN. Well, let's say we are repeating ourselves every so often… you'd still imagine that we're bound to come across some resemblance to truth, right?

DAVE. It'll come down to energy, I think?

JOHN. How do you mean?

DAVE. Whether we have the energy to keep on going until we find out what it is we're searching for. I can't be doing this indefinitely, you know!

JOHN. What are you talking about! I've got a gun! Of course you can!

DAVE. When I get too tired, John?! What happens then?

JOHN. Do you feel close to that?

DAVE. I'm closer. Each time I'm getting a little closer.

JOHN. And you're worried you'll be too tired to talk?

DAVE. I'm worried you'll shoot me in the face.

JOHN. Good.

DAVE. Have you started to fantasise about the time when we eventually reach the truth?

JOHN. What?

DAVE. I have.

JOHN. When do you find the time to do that?

DAVE. During.

JOHN. What?

DAVE. As we're…

JOHN. As we're telling the story?!

DAVE. Only sometimes!

JOHN. You're thinking about a moment of peace while we're supposed to be busy searching for what might get us there!?

DAVE. Is that wrong?

JOHN. Well, it's not very diligent, Dave! A strict man would say that it's shoddy work practice! Shouldn't you be concentrating wholly?!

DAVE. The brain wanders.

JOHN. Well, is it any wonder it's taking us all this time when you've got your sights on the prize! Stick to the details, Dave. Isn't that the problem with people?! They have no concern for 'the now'.

JOHN. I have concern for 'the now'! I am doing my best, you know.

DAVE. A little more concentration would help.

DAVE. But what happens when I run out of words?

JOHN. Impossible.

DAVE. Is it?

JOHN. Think about it. It's impossible to run out of words. At least we have that to be thankful for.

DAVE. Shit. Do you think I can leave for a few moments, John? Go outside for a walk or something.

JOHN *holds the gun towards* DAVE*'s face.*

JOHN (*prompting*). 'It seemed right that it would be the anniversary...'

DAVE. Please.

JOHN. Are you fucking stupid! CARRY ON!

JOHN *presses the gun hard against* DAVE*'s forehead.*

A pause.

DAVE. Did we have a conversation as to whether we believed there was a bullet in the gun?

A pause.

JOHN. I'm not too sure.

DAVE. Do you think there's a bullet in there?

JOHN. It's safer to believe that there might be a bullet.

DAVE. I probably decided that some time ago.

JOHN. I expect you did.

Long pause.

DAVE. I really have to stop some time, you know.

A pause.

JOHN. Start.

DAVE *then continues with* JOHN *pointing the gun to his face.*

DAVE. It seemed right that it would be the anniversary. Seemed almost too perfect that today would have to be the day. Would have to be the same day a year on from the time you first saw her. How ordered it all was.

JOHN. How simple and true and right.

DAVE. How simple and true and right.

JOHN. Good.

DAVE. Like the very first time you saw her in the park drinking her drink… like you gave life to her somehow.

JOHN. Like she just existed from that moment on. Like I just imagined her and there she was, taking her drink on the park bench that evening right in front of me. Looking at the little quack-quacks neither interested nor disinterested. Just blank-looking.

DAVE. She looked blank to you and just then you realised that this is what attracted you to her.

JOHN. Her blankness.

DAVE. And as you followed her home that night from the park and followed her the next morning and afternoon you gave her different personalities, didn't you?

JOHN. Yes.

DAVE. The same way you did to the hundreds of blank people you had followed about town. And in certain angles, certain lights, she became different people from your past.

JOHN. Right.

DAVE. And by the end of the first week and after following her in and out of the shops and the parks and on and off buses… and as you looked at her sitting on the park bench and taking her drink and looking blankly at those little quack-quacks… you decided there and then who she was to you. You decided you were looking at your…?

DAVE *stops and waits.* JOHN *responds:*

JOHN. My friend Dave.

A pause. DAVE *stunned.* JOHN *too is a little surprised.*

I decided I was looking at my friend Dave.

DAVE *continues uneasily.*

DAVE. The young woman you had followed that first week and was following every week since... meant this to you?

JOHN. Yes.

DAVE. She was maybe going about her own life but what was important was that she was Dave to you. Simple. So as you showered that morning and walked around your flat, unconnected images and stories all featuring you and Dave seemed to follow you. Traces of Dave started to stink up one room making you walk to another room.

JOHN. As a little boy I'd be up early. Woken with a sick stomach and sat at the kitchen table facing the soggy cornflakes and Dave already sat there talking to my dad. Sat there dressed in neatness. Skin buffed clean and hair parted tidy and Dad and Dave talking the insurance talk.

DAVE. You hated that insurance talk and 'cause that's all that your father spoke... you hated your father.

JOHN. Hated his fucking guts, Dave!

DAVE. But as much as you hated your father it was your best friend Dave you hated more.

JOHN. But *why*?

DAVE. You'd use the morning to investigate this question. Today being the day it was... it was important to remind yourself of all the reasons you hated Dave. *Can we stop this?!*

JOHN. If I was going to do what I was going to do... I would have to be certain and revisit those terrible moments of my life with Dave for this one last time. I took in some fresh air in the outside and started to spell out all these terrible moments in clear embarrassing details.

DAVE. John, please...!

JOHN *slams* DAVE*'s head onto the table and presses the gun hard against him.*

JOHN. As a little boy in my house my mother would follow
Dave about in her underwear. The only friend I ever brought
home and Mother's in her bra and knickers pressing her
crotch against Dave's arm. I scream at Mother and she pulls
down my trousers and smacks my bare backside with a coat
hanger. Dave sat watching in the corner with a glass of hot
milk. Watching and smiling. Smiling and watching!

DAVE. That's not true…!

JOHN. It's the day of my tenth birthday but Dave's at a
neighbour's cocktail party and dressed like a miniature man
in his black tuxedo and my mother's flirting with Dave and
saying to the others, 'I've got rid of the husband for the
night and here's my date! Isn't Dave handsome? Isn't he a
hunk?' While I'm sitting at home beneath the stairs with
my photo album and cutting the head off Dave. Dave the
Fuck! And that time I'm at the supermarket. My teenage
body jammed into a pair of tennis shorts and I see Dave
next to the fish fingers with the girl I love. A little sneer
stuck on Dave's face and the girl I love laughing at my
shorts. My mind was settled and for the afternoon I focused
again on the young woman I was following this past year.
The young woman who had come to represent Dave to me.
The young woman who was Dave's old sweetheart and my
only love…

DAVE. Fuck!

JOHN. That evening, just as I planned…

DAVE. John, is this…

JOHN. SAY IT!

DAVE (*shaken*). That evening, just as you planned it, you'd talk
to her about the lake and the ducks and the wonderful simple
life of the duck. You would hear her voice until you finally
decided not to hear her voice any more. To stop her voice
and keep it forever stuck in the simple words of ducks.

JOHN *continues slowly.*

JOHN. Already in my mind I have returned home from the park, Dave. I'm inside my flat and neither tense nor calm, Dave. I move about with a glass of wine feeling the carpet on the soles of my feet, Dave. I ignore the little grass stains on my trousers, the slight tear on my shirt sleeves and feel pleased that no blood has marked me. And it's like I'm reborn somehow... or perhaps yet born. In doing what I did I've erased the images of my best friend from my past. Those wicked stories I've dragged around all these years. Dave both ceases to exist or ever exist to me. In the morning I will wake up and start a new life. In the morning the ducks will find Dave's sweetheart's dead body in the bushes... and now it will be their time to look blankly at her.

JOHN *lets go of* DAVE *and* DAVE *sits up, very anxious.* JOHN *calmly puts down the gun and suddenly there's an ease to him.* DAVE *needs an answer.*

DAVE. Is this the truth? Is it close to the truth, John?!

A pause.

JOHN. I can't be sure.

A pause.

DAVE. But the truth doesn't matter to us, does it?

JOHN. Doesn't it?

A pause.

DAVE. The exact truth hardly matters, John.

A pause.

JOHN. Then we're searching for what exactly?

DAVE. Difficult to say. But we are most definitely searching for something other than what we have.

DAVE *quickly picks up the gun and places it back in* JOHN*'s hand. He raises it and holds* JOHN*'s hand in position. The gun back up against his head where it belongs.* DAVE *continues.*

Static begins to fade up slowly.

It seemed right that it would be the anniversary. Seemed almost too perfect that today would have to be the day. Would have to be the same day a year on from the time when you first saw her. How ordered it all it was…

The static fills the auditorium and we watch DAVE *continue.* JOHN *then takes his hand away and* DAVE *is left holding the gun against his own head as he talks frantically.* JOHN *just sits back and looks at him for a moment. Nowhere to go,* JOHN *takes the gun back off* DAVE *and keeps it pointed at* DAVE's *head.*

This all lasts for forty-five seconds.

Sound cuts and blackout.

The End.

THE SMALL THINGS

The Small Things was first performed by Paines Plough as part of the 'This Other England' season at the Menier Chocolate Factory, London, on 28 January 2005. The cast was as follows:

WOMAN	Valerie Lilley
MAN	Bernard Gallagher
Director	Vicky Featherstone
Designer	Neil Warmington
Lighting Designer	Natasha Chivers
Sound Designer	Mat Ort

Characters

MAN

WOMAN

Heavy red-velvet curtains open slowly to the sound of a loud dramatic drum roll on timpani drums.

At the front of the large stage are two armchairs beside each other, sort of faced towards each other.

In one of them sits an elderly MAN, *his age indecipherable, his face worn and tired. He wears a cardigan and a shirt and bow tie. His trousers a little worn. Surprisingly, he wears a very polished pair of small black children's shoes with red laces. His expression like a bemused clown. He holds a battered wind-up clock and stares at it.*

In the other armchair is an old tape recorder.

To the left and behind the MAN, *a* WOMAN *sits at a small oak table with a lace tablecloth, polishing twelve small ceramic animals lined up in a row. Her age again difficult for us to gauge, her face a little tired and loose. She wears a housecoat over a plain skirt and blouse and a pair of slippers. Similarly to the* MAN, *in front of her is a wind-up clock, though hers is immaculate.*

On the back wall of the stage is an enormous window/screen. A yellow-grey light emanates from it and light moves slowly in and out of shadow like cloud passing.

The two sit for a while doing very little as the sound of the drums continues loud.

She looks over towards the window.

The drum roll suddenly stops with a flourish.

WOMAN (*to the window*). Window. Knick-knacks. Song.

His clock sounds. He slaps it off and begins.

MAN. It's been raining for the past two weeks which would account for dampness. Not that I could remember. How could I remember. Impossible to remember! But dampness is there, its cause forgotten but dampness is everywhere. My shoes on the parquet floor and Mother's shoes in front. We're marching me and her. Parquet floor zigzagging down corridors. I understand my damp hands as fear and I'm sort of crying. I had cried in car but forgotten I was upset. But in crying now I remember the tears of before and remember that this day's primary feelings are fear, you see. Fear. Each salty tear a reminder, each clammy hand putting me in my place. Mother's heels on hard floor, anxious. Marking out seconds. They're alternating 'tween her tight breath and beat of heels. The clip clop, the tight breath. The clip clop. My breath.

He pants three times and stops.

I'm three years old and all talk is me and future and books and learning and I'd be lying if I said I wasn't excited because in truth I'm dead excited. I'm leaving behind a life that's somewhat lumpen – HEY!

He stops and suddenly writes in a small notebook with a pencil.

Fine word 'lumpen'. A single rhyme with pumpkin, love. (*Closes the notebook.*) For what are babies but lumps. Happy lumps granted but lumpen and sat still all day much like I am sat right now. Difference 'tween babies and me, is lumpen babies must give in to life while my giving in will be to death. One a cheery departure and one not so cheery… though in honesty which one is which. Slight joke. No need for slight jokes when no one's laughing, the bastards! The clip clop stops. She kneels in front of me. She hugs me. She kisses me on cheek. Starts telling me to enjoy my day but all this time I'm looking right down her blouse. I never loved my mother in that way. Never had feelings of… feelings of lust… too strong, easy now… lust?!!… feelings of…? I know what I mean! Frankly she was never very loving to me. That hug in the classroom an unusual show of affection more to do with doing right thing than telling me of her love, self-pity, very attractive in an old man.

He laughs. She laughs.

Oh, very good! Very nice!

They both stop laughing.

I drop my school bag and reach in and hold my mother's breasts.

WOMAN. Oh!

MAN. It's an action that lasts all of a split second and at first I'm amazed that the motion is so fluid for a three year old and that I make contact so precisely and also that in my hands both titties weigh exact same measure. This is my moment! Beginning of my professional life. Yes! Before she slaps my hands away and belts me across head, before my new classmates burst into laughter and I start my journey into a childhood of ridicule and psychological torture, not true, though interesting! Before any of this shite and it's just me with Mother's tits held in perfect symmetry in my hands... at that moment I promise myself a life in engineering. I am ready... for order.

He looks at the clock. She's looking at her clock.

WOMAN. I'm up out of bed and flinging myself through house like a mad thing, like a rag doll. And downstairs dragging sweaty fingers down walls. Into kitchen and a breakfast scene. Dozy-chat mixing with pop music off radio – ding-a-ling. Cornflakes crunching above the quiet din of breakfast time and all is a deadly normal but for Dad's face. Dad's face! Crikey! He's been complaining about a headache for the past month! Last week Mother caught him staring at the clouds, staring at the birds and shaking his head and mumbling to himself, 'What chaos in the world. What terrible chaos.' I saw him walking around town in dead straight lines while all around the world is going about the day-to-day business of accident and chance. Accident and chance, them two words churning Dad's stomach. This morning and his eyes are stuck out of his face like they want to be rid of his head. Still sat in his jim-jams he pours the cornflakes out onto table, sits there and starts to count them out one by one. Sets out cornflakes into a neat square and my brother starts to giggle. An orange square and the disorder of the cornflakes are set to a pattern, you see. Well, skip forward to dinner time, still sat in his jim-jams and he has us whispering our words. No dinner sounds and us all hushed and careful. He wipes the sauce off his spaghetti and lays spaghetti out into a simple grid-shape and for the first time we hear these new words, 'Where would any of us be without order, kids?'

MAN. Christ.

WOMAN. Suddenly it's us who's starting each day wondering where we'd be without order. What terrible shape the world would be if the great Lord hadn't such an appreciation for ordered things? 'Sending night after day and autumn to cool summer and all of those happy miracles.' Six years old and I thought that, then. Because of my father's persistence, order starts ruling the house. For one year timetables meet us each morning. Two watches for two naughty children laid out on table. Each task allotted time. An exact time for each task. Strap watches on and we slot into our routine. Can't remember exact times now. No, can't. Not important. Hardly adds to the story! But the shape of the day. The rhythm of how it runs and how I run. A bloody odd sight, I tell ya! Two children, timetables alert being pushed about house by seconds, by minutes. And Father standing a foot behind always guiding and watching. 'Watching and guiding! Watching and guiding!' My four-year-old brother spends too long washing the dishes and I'm looking at my father standing over him screaming at the back of his head. Not words just this long scream, right here.

She indicates where on the head and screams.

MAN. Easy.

WOMAN. The day after that there was no timetables out. Mother sat in bed with Father, 'Things will be all right, Martin.' At night I can hear him sobbing and saying how sorry he is that he screamed at my brother but really we'd be lost without our timetables. Lost without 'the order of the routine, Maureen.' And it's true, at first I am lost! No timetable and I stand in house searching for routine. It's me

who's stood behind my brother now and screaming at the
back of his head. Monkey see monkey do. In this little scene
the familiar feeling safe strangely. (*Screams. Stops*.) Safe but
wrong, surely, what with my brother's tears. I start panicking
a little and face my stopwatch and counting the seconds as
they leave me. Useless and stood still and unable to figure
out the day. But at least there's order in the seconds, hey?!
One two three four five six and so on... At least some pattern
to keep safe!

MAN. Yap yap yap!

WOMAN. I'm sitting on the couch dead still and silent and
watching the seconds and holding my breath for fear that my
breath might blow the seconds to God knows where! It's the
worry of the uncertain, as Dad might say. You start an action
that effects another and then another and pretty soon life
turns into chaos. 'Look at them clouds! Formless and
blowing about! It's bloody anarchy up there!' So it's best to
keep inside and sat on couch and do nothing at all. Well, fuck
that! I have to stop those thoughts because that's where
madness lies and Mother says that one mad person in house
is bad enough and it's best to go outside and investigate the
village like any other normal girl should. Which I do. (*About
a small ceramic cat*.) Now this is the fella I talk to!

MAN. Were you listening to my first story?

WOMAN. All of them I talk to at some stage, of course.

MAN. Wasn't it short on detail today?

WOMAN. Not conversations obviously for really it's all one
way, don't be daft.

MAN. Hey?

WOMAN. It's always one-way conversations with me and my
knick-knacks, isn't it, boys! But you know I stopped talking
to them because of... (*Stops*.) Actually I can't remember
why I stopped talking to them. (*Rattled*.) Boredom, of
course, but that's no reason. Boredom's not a good enough
reason. Sure boredom's got the run of me, hasn't it! Beyond

boredom I am and shaped from a much more boring place than just your everyday run-of-the-mill, 'Fuck me, I'm bored!' So it's not likely that it could be boredom. Though you never know. Doesn't seem likely or logical, mind you.

MAN (*staring at the clock and shaking it*). Tickatockatick-atocktickatockatickatocktickatockatickatock!

WOMAN. Seems strange that I would stop talking to the knick-knacks, doesn't it? Christ, I'll have to rectify that one and slot it back into the day. Once it's not taking away from the stories! Once the clock and the stories allow for some idle chit-chat with the knick-knacks then where's the harm, do you get me?!

MAN. Not really.

WOMAN. But, anyway, *this* fella I talked to on account of his inquisitive face. Ya cheeky! Look at that! He always has a cleverer look than me. Especially. At. This. Very. Moment.

Silence as they do very little. Suddenly the sound of the timpani drum as it builds to a flourish. It stops.

His clock sounds again and he slams it off and resumes.

MAN. I leave my house and slam the front door with an imprint of Mother's hand on face.

WOMAN (*looking at clock*). What?

MAN. Little stiffness still in pants. My short pants. The pants that dug into my prick on account of new zip. The second-hand zip, yes Mother, removed from somewhere or other and welded onto these shorts and making my summer-life a misery, by the way. Yes misery, Mother! A chafing misery! This morning worst than normal, though, because of the stiffness. My six-year-old stiffness pressed against zip.

WOMAN (*staring at her clock. Sighs*). Fine.

MAN. I was sat on bed with Mother's bra laid out in front of me. Her room and it was the mothball smells that had me in a daze for I couldn't hear her feet – clip clop – on the stairs for everything was that lovely bra. Well, I had just placed my face into one of the cups of the lovely bra… when bloody door flies open and Mother's hand 'Schmack! Schmack! Schmack!', me running for the door, for the front door then and outside outside-outside-outside-outside-outside-outside…

WOMAN. And outside to village for me and, 'Oh, isn't it great to be finally in the outside!' – skip skip – with conversations… conversations about absolutely nothing. I stand there for minutes with all talk leading to nowhere, imagine that! All order is bent out of shape in the outside. The world made up of this small talk and listening to the words trail off to… wherever words go to. To nothing maybe. To nowhere maybe. To… to… (*Reprimanding herself.*) I really mustn't think those thoughts and get back! Chin up, woman. You allow Mister Glum inside you'll be booking your ticket to that road down below, the bastard. 'Where's this you're off to?'

MAN. Out. Just out.

WOMAN. Your mother's well, isn't she?

MAN. She is, yeah. She's fine.

WOMAN. You look nice. A little dressed up, mind you. Chit-chat.

MAN. They're my Sunday clothes.

WOMAN. Are you off to Church Fête then?

MAN. I am as a matter of fact. Chit-chat chit-chat.

WOMAN. Off to Church Fête?

MAN. Chit-chat chit-chat. (*He laughs.*)

MAN *and* WOMAN. Chit-chat chit-chat. Chit-chat chit-chat. Chit-chat chit-chat. Chit-chat chit-chat. Chit-chat chit-chat.

WOMAN (*laughing*). She can see where I'm at and where I'm off to! A plate full of meringues, look!! With cellophane all wrapped them, woman!?

MAN (*quiet*). Tick tock tick tock.

WOMAN. It's not like I'm off directly to the new swimming pool, is it?! Got me inflatable armbands for that job! Won't get far in the pool wearing these meringues, will I?! Bottom of the swimming pool with the meringues! How could you forget about them meringues?

MAN. Meringues can never be forgotten.

WOMAN. Sure that silly cow was just making the small talk, bless her. The sound of this village played out in everyone's words, hey. Maybe only fifty of us livin' here and our voices all stuck in same music. Close my eyes, it's like listening to myself as I walk through village. Skipping through broken chit-chat towards Fête in field at back of church.

MAN. What time do you think it is?

WOMAN. Ohh the lovely sound of those words and the shape of the small talk! And days have their very own sound, don't they?! The way people talk on the Sunday decidedly different from the Friday talk. One all restless and shapeless, the other a little languid somehow. Fantastic word 'languid'. I'll use it again before the day runs out.

The clock sounds its alarm again and again he slams it off.

MAN. I am stood at the big table...

WOMAN. Languid. Genius.

MAN. ... my eyes full of cakes and buns. I'm looking at different shapes of cakes with a young engineer's critical eye. My mouth's already bubbling up with spit, with expectation for the cream, for the sponge. I didn't have breakfast this morning so even the shortbread's looking half decent, though structurally a little unsound, not true, no matter, carry on! But then I see the meringues! Those lovely magnificent gable-shaped cakes!

Slight pause.

It's not lost on me that yet again it's Mother's breasts I'm thinking about as I look down on those meringues... so I buy two... shove one in my mouth.

WOMAN. The meringue's halfway in and that's when you look at me.

A pause.

MAN (*to himself. Whispers*). Meringues.

A pause.

WOMAN. My mother made them.

MAN. Did she? Crikey. They're lovely.

WOMAN. I helped her to.

MAN. Did ya? You did a good job. They're delicious. How come I haven't seen you about village chit-chat?

WOMAN. My dad likes to keep us locked inside house. That's all finished, though. From hereon in, I'm outside house.

MAN. What about a dip in that new swimming pool?

WOMAN. And you're dragging me by the hand and pulling the arm off me! The words too fast in your mouth spitting out all the things you're about to do in life. Into swimming pool and the voices of other children smacking off the tiles and you and me strippin' off into our underpants. You jabbering on about this and that! And it's like my last year locked in the house and stuck in Dad's routines is soon forgotten. My childhood returned with your talk of life and loves and hates. Christ but you're a talker!

MAN. I can't stop talking, me! I'm like my Auntie Ada! A woman who wore her teeth out with all her chat. Who had a jaw the size of a small car with all that bloody talk. Never held hands with a girl before so in its excitement my brain is packing bullshit into my gob. I'm all 'me this' and 'me that'! I'm coming across as a right little pain in the arse. Zip into shop and buy some penny chews just to bung me up but I can't stop the talk! You bobbing along beside, your little blue eyes smiling at me all innocent yet cheeky. We're into pool and I'm strippin' off my pants like a mad thing. Six years old I'm already thinking of us sharing a bed and making babies, getting married and getting the decorators in. What's got into me!? I'm thinking all this but talking structural engineering all of a sudden. I have to stop talking and get splashing. Get splashing!

WOMAN. Into pool then with these nicked inflatable armbands and aren't we skinny. The cold water goosebumping our little arms, look!

MAN. I look like I'm made from chicken! Isn't skin a wonder all the same?!

WOMAN. We're facing each other doing the doggy paddle and you cross your eyes and make a face. Momentarily I think you've gone spastic on me but that soon passes and you're smiling once more like a normal child.

MAN. I never was one for comedy but always felt the need to give it a go.

WOMAN. You can't stop talking, can ya! You're like a factory for words and I can't stop smiling at ya!

MAN. I'm Auntie bloody Ada, that's who!

He laughs a little.

WOMAN. The pool clears and we're left alone, hey.

A pause. Slower.

We're like the last two people alive, me and you. We imagine we are. We think about us being the last two and what fun we might have in that world. We don't say much and just bob about.

MAN. Truth is, my six-year-old jaw's all worn out from the chat and the penny chews. Feels good to stay quiet for a bit.

Long pause.

Dried off now and we walk back outside to the sun and the lure of the Church Fête and those meringues on the cake table.

WOMAN. Walk side by side and the conversation settling into this easy rhythm. You're less of the jabbering spastic and I'm finding words I never thought I had. Our words equal fold around each other and I suppose we're at ease now. It's all good. It's all...? nice.

Slight pause.

That day we're bonded me and you. The day of the no timetable. The day of the no stopwatch. The day of the no routine.

Slight pause.

We're standing back at the cake table.

Slight pause.

Dad's standing next to me suddenly. Takes me by the hand.

A pause.

His knuckles are bruised and bloody.

She turns away from the clock.

MAN. I've been thinking about other things so much that maybe it's started this...? 'thing'. Seems possible that all these new thoughts may be the cause of what's happening inside. Not sure who it is talking inside of me. Give him a name and you prove he's alive... so not quite ready to give who it is inside a name just yet?

Looks at his hands and whispers.

I'm no longer six years old... nor twelve even... that much is true. Are you listening to me?

A pause.

WOMAN. Yes.

MAN. How can I be sure?

A pause.

WOMAN. I'm here, aren't I?

MAN. Yeah but how can I be certain you're listening?

WOMAN. Good question.

He looks down at his clock. He resumes.

MAN. You leave with your dad.

Slight pause.

I see the other children run into woods and it's like my legs take me after them. All squealing inside with trees and us all busy, all fast. No order inside there. Time bent out of shape. Our world given over to blurry browns and gold and laughter. (*Whispers.*) Nice words them.

A pause.

He's lying face down, his clothes off him. We get a big stick and roll his body over. Dead leaves stuck on his front like some fancy vest. His blood black, his fingers thick with muck, his face smashed up but we all know him well. His father owns chip shop in the village and he works there on Saturdays. His mouth open… you can see his teeth smashed up from the thumping he got.

Slight pause.

The chip-shop man has killed his only son. Cut out his tongue and smashed him up.

Slight pause.

He gave me a free battered sausage once.

WOMAN (*staring at clock*). What time do you think it is?

MAN. I think I'll sit a while and listen to him talking inside a me.

WOMAN (*quietly. Excited*). That time.

MAN. I'll decide whether it's time to give him a name and be done with it all. (*Whispers.*) I'll decide whether it's time to give him a name and be done with this life.

Slight pause.

Do I really mean what I say…? or have these words got the run of me completely?

He's frightened now. Snaps.

Fuck it.

The MAN *closes his eyes but immediately opens them and stares down at his clock.*

Tentatively, the WOMAN *turns the face of the clock away from her. She breathes a sigh of relief.*

WOMAN. Just before going to the window I torture myself with a little silence! Which isn't very nice and a bit difficult but nature calls for a pause. Such is sleep. When sleep finally arrives – lazy bastard. You can't move forward lest you stop now and again, can ya? Take stock. Otherwise it's just moving willy-nilly. Take these little fellas. A constant polish just wears them out. Better to let dust settle. Ya can't be handling the knick-knacks willy-nilly, can you? Wear out the little beggers. Give them a breath. A little standstill. Just look at that face on the inquisitive one. Right? Yeah? Well aware he is of my next move so why the questioning face? I've got every right to wipe that look right off ya, ya little! Anyway, as much as I try for silence I seem to fall short on account of this talking.

A pause. She looks over to the window and smiles a little.

Right about this time I allow myself some action!

She stands up from her seat. A little uneasy, she waits until she has her balance.

Nothing in the world quite like a little action to get the blood racing.

She then walks very slowly towards the window. Whispers to herself.

Window window window! Suddenly 'possibility' shows its happy head.

Slight pause.

Now look how I walk, sweetheart. My speed... lack of... position of my head bent towards floor... body a little

tight… in… in… in…? it may look like constipation… it is
in fact in anticipation. Hardly my greatest performance but
it's found me nearing the window once again. The window.
My look then! My look…? my look a little hungry at first,
probably. It is the window after all and not the deadness of
the walls. Warrants some joy. It does offer… a perspective,
definitely, what window doesn't?!… and dare I say a bigger
hope. Try to ignore my dodgy legs as they root me to this
floor, raising the head to look towards and out of the window
like a fat man acknowledging a meat supper…

Finally she looks out the window.

… and there it is! The house in the distance on top of that
mountain. Our two houses blinking over at each other… over
the…? (*Thinks.*) Oh, the world that was there, that's enough.
That silent road below. The sea.

Slight pause.

Small house much like this house. Wooden-panelled, same as
this – very nice. Mind you, I haven't seen the outside of this
place for an age and it may be covered in another form for
all I know. Ice-cream wafers! (*Laughs a little.*) Hardly. But
that house. I can sometimes see a figure sitting by the…

A pause as she looks out.

I can imagine all sorts of life in that house. Lively chit-chat
as the night gets closer. Music. I should have never burnt that
piano! Other things could have been burnt. The bloody
knick-knacks, for example! What music do they give me but
the daily inquisition. The daily reminder! The piano was an
innocent. Day I arrived in here… it was there, sat in the
corner, all wise and full of history and loved once most
certainly. I tried playing it for the first few months but it was
bloody murder. Fel' like music itself was dying. Like these
sausage fingers were drumming out the death march! Well, if
it wasn't for the tape recorder, wasn't for your song,
sweetheart, I might have felt like all music was six foot
under! Getting ahead of myself! No mention of the song
before before… easy easy easy! But that house. Come on!!
Come on!!

Slight pause. Covering her ears and concentrating.

Such music there. Something lively now. Something that would give my veins a good draining, the floorboards a pounding... a celebration for...? Well, not for anything in particular but for the sake of a difference... a different life... something...? can the word 'frivolous' still be used despite everything? I don't see why not! Something frivolous is happening in that house. Something frivolous is happening!

Laughs a little. A pause.

It was only the one figure I saw, mind... and now gone... mustn't get too glum, come on! CHRIST! We all know where glum gets me... a longer day for starters. I mean, I do have some fun times in here. Hardly a holiday camp, granted, but we do have the odd giggle, don't we, sweetheart, hey? Remember that day when you... and it was... and you did that... and I was... and before we know it... it was all...

She laughs. The MAN *remains silent. She suddenly stops laughing.*

(*Downbeat.*) Oh, it's too easy to wear out these glorious moments by the window! Enough then.

She turns away from the window and walks back to her seat.

MAN (*looks down at his shoes*). Look how they remind me. These! These funny children's shoes. All these years... just following me.

The timpani drum roll begins to fade up.

Reminding me...

The drum roll finishes with a flourish. His clock sounds and again he slaps it off and resumes.

'But I don't want sauce, I like them salty.' 'Sauce is salty, ya daft bugger!' 'They make the chips soggy like slugs.' 'What's wrong with slugs? Are you being a naughty boy?' My little heartbeat then. And him and me know what he's talking about. Find myself saying 'brown'. Fixes me with his look and covers my chips in that brown tangy shite and turning the chips to slugs. He's backing me into the wall now and him holding my soggy chips and joking about his naughty son who needed silence the other day, didn't he, who needed the routine like the boss man said. 'But stood up against his own dad!' So then kicked in, weren't he! Kicked in! I watch the chip-shop man take t'street outside with this new power. He walks the road and it's like he sucks in all life about him. Holds my soggy chips up to the sky and fucks them against a shop window. It's his time, it's his time.

She looks at her clock.

WOMAN. I'm sat in living room listening to Father and the chip-shop man. And Father's big idea they talk. They talk about spreading the silence. How quiet and peaceful the village will be without words. How perfect the world without this chit-chat. Over a cup of tea they speak about the naughty boy and how they sliced his tongue off. My timetable they gave him and the routine that kept him. The routine making him. For a week my timetable marking this boy's every breath 'til he stood up. 'So kicked in, weren't he. Kicked in.' I look at Mother looking at Dad's bruised and bloody knuckles. And her too bashed down to talk up. Her words are stuck in her throat as she carves up the coffee cake. It starts. It begins.

MAN. Mother pulls me aside – clip clop clip clop – and tells me now's the time to grow up fast. She tells me not to be scared. But I am scared. 'Don't be scared, love.' 'I'm scared of the chip-shop man.' Strikes me across face, throws her hands to her eyes and she's the one who cries! Well, fuck this, I'm outside-outside-outside-outside-outside...

WOMAN. And just me and you alone in village walking towards each other and a secret I have to tell.

MAN. Something's happening here.

WOMAN. It's my dad and the chip-shop man. Only the bad ones will be silenced, so don't be scared?

MAN. 'But I am scared!' And walk through woods and pass where they took up the boy's body. Instead of him there, someone has put a bunch of flowers. I bend down and pick up a red carnation and hand it to ya. A romantic gesture for a six-year-old. Though in hindsight a jot morbid.

WOMAN. Take my hand then and let's walk down to river at the other end of woods.

MAN. Each step and another month and a year passes. For six years I'm by your side.

WOMAN. Six years it passes with my dad and the chip-shop man slicing the tongues.

MAN. And we talk about those ten people who've been silenced already. We watch them walk about the village with clipboards and stopwatches. They walk in little trenches the chip-shop man dug. Like train tracks the trenches are and stuck in patterns the Silent shuffle along all funny-looking. We laugh about the routines they're given. An alarm sounds and we see a man stood outside a house and made to count the bricks. Another man stood behind this man made to count the seconds it takes the man to count the bricks. An alarm sounds and we see a woman stand in a field counting bees, counting birds, counting flies, a man made to measure all that can be measured in the village. Another man marking the time it takes this man to measure these things 'til that's his order for every day after. An alarm sounds and I see a woman made to count her breaths in a single day making that number of breaths her marker for all of her days. An alarm sounds...

WOMAN. Shhhh.

He covers his mouth with his hands, stopping the words. A pause. He lowers his hands.

We sit in our spot. Two little twelve-year-olds by river's edge. Turn away from what the village's been turned into and we lose ourselves in our secret chat. Our talk all shapeless and trailing off to where ever words go to. Just talk nonsense talk, really. The sort of talk that has my dad feeling sick. Talk ourselves stupid 'til we give into silence. In these moments by the river we happily give into silence.

MAN. A kiss.

WOMAN. And kiss then. And lie down into autumn leaves you
set up like a mattress. The little light about us too, a jigsaw
of browns and golds, isn't it? All talk is gone with your easy
breath against my stomach. The river sounds led by your
breath. I sleep. Lost in a dream of some happy house on a
mountain… they were my dreams back then. I'm sleeping.

MAN (*grimaces*). That will be my insides scheming. Whatever
they're saying it takes me by the second. I try to listen but
the talking is buried deep. Might I be able to hear it soon?
For right now I wonder the purpose of this telling once
again.

A pause.

Still.

He stares down at his clock and silently mouths as the
seconds pass until he must speak again. Quietly then.

You sleep with the river sounds led by your breath. The little
currents whirring all easy, the popping sounds ebbing up and
down. I turn and look towards river.

Slight pause.

I'm looking at the chip-shop man standing right by your
mother and he's pulling at her hair. She's kneeling in the
water and her eyes staring right over at me. Those ten others
who are already silenced are stood by the bank looking on all
dumb with clipboards and stopwatches. He takes a kitchen
knife to her tongue. Blood all down her pinny and he shoves
her under the water. Your dad drags her out and holds her up
to the others like some wet puppy.

Slight pause.

'Reborn,' he says. All polite applause. Little applause. Your
mother's looking over at me. The Silent are looking at us.

WOMAN. Right about this time I remind myself to stay
happy! Well, not happy! Don't be ridiculous! Happy!
(*Laughs.*) What's the word? (*She can't think of it.*) Now
don't fail me. Christ, imagine that nightmare! Each second
passing and another word abandons ship and then where

would I be? Stuck in goo-gaa words. The brain turned to slush and me the picture of old age. Little dribble out side of mouth and mumbling out the inane! Little dusty smells crawling out my backside unannounced! Shuffling across lino with all the speed of slugs! Hah! Actually closer to that image than I'd like to be. But right about this time I remind myself to stay 'confident'. Confident for what reason? Now there's a question. The question. 'Cause without confidence bloody fear would gobble me up and then where would I be? Where would I be would not be here. Here looking out window, across at that house and hoping for… it doesn't matter what for, 'cause really hope is enough to go on. 'To go on'? To survive by. Hope is certainly more than enough to survive by. I've made it that way and to be honest I am of an age to know nothing else – hint of pity in that voice! There is only the chance of fear and the hope for something marginally better than this existence. A moment of honesty. (*Disciplining herself.*) 'Honesty'!! STOP TALKING! STOP IT!

A pause.

It's time to turn that frown to upside down. Not the song just yet but the knick-knacks! Many moons ago I happened upon another purpose for these fellas. A purpose a lot more creative than being the recipients of a good dusting every fifteen minutes. I made a show for them. The story was…? such and such. I had an ending but I threw it out. It didn't seem worthy of the start. But I did like it though and it grew on me, so I got rid of the start and was left with ending which seemed unsatisfactory now that it didn't have a beginning.

MAN (*groans*). Oh my God.

WOMAN. Without a start or an ending there was absolutely no reason to continue. But of course I did!

MAN. Of course.

WOMAN. For there will always be a reason. Though for the life of me I have no idea what it was chit-chat chit-chat! Anyway, every day… I take a minute out to wait for the knick-knacks to begin from 'the middle'. Free my mind of these stories and thoughts of madness and just… wait.

Long pause as she sits and stares at them.

Nothing just yet. A little stage-struck even now, bless 'em.

Long pause as she waits.

And still nothing just yet.

Another long pause as she stares waiting for the knick-knacks.

Still nothing.

Another long pause. Finally her optimism breaks.

(*Quiet.*) Nothing.

MAN. When did this body stop? When I say this body, I mean the legs, of course. The rest is still intact and in order. Reasonably. But these chicken legs gave up the chase a little time ago. Body's way of telling me to stay put and think things through. Which I have been doing, thank you very much! Which has become my everything. This thinking things through. But why not just other thoughts? The here and the now. Luxury. Her about me and fussing about me and making my tea… of course, there's never any tea… but us lost in our chit-chat, you know. Why not only these small things?

Slight pause.

I'll whisper so the shoes can't listen.

Slight pause. He whispers slowly.

Am I ready… to give in? Am I ready… to be silenced?

His clocks sounds and he wrestles with it and then sits on it to block out the noise.

Looking at her clock she resumes.

WOMAN. We're sat on the couch eating chips. Mother standing in the corner where the telly was. She's faced towards wall like a bad girl. I'm watching her pudgy hands shaking by her

side, little snivelling noises from her silent gob. She's heard
something from Dad and the chip-shop man. She knows why
we're in our swimming togs and waiting this past hour. Me
and my brother sat there eating the soggy chips and thinking
about the swimming pool. Oh, it has to be the swimming
pool. No other reason for this baggy swimsuit. Fuck it, I look
like I'm sheddin' skin. The crotch that baggy, I'm a little
undecent to be honest. Little breasts like garden peas, I'm a
right state!

The MAN*'s clock has stopped and, delighted, he takes it
back into his hands and shakes it in triumph.*

MAN. YES!

WOMAN. We're outside with Dad marching behind us. I look
at my little brother still juggling with his chips. The brown
sauce spitting onto his belly and he's dead excited! 'You love
the swimming pool, don't ya? Into your inflatable tortoise
and you'll be in the pool 'til Christmas.' My little feet
pinching on the road. We're walking over all those trenches
that are dug for those Silent Ones. Father, the big engine,
marching us down street, 'Where would any of us be without
order? What greatness this silence. What wonder the
routine.' Blah blah blah BLAH BLAH BLAH BLAH BLAH
BLAH BLAH BLAH! WE WALK!

The MAN*'s clock sounds and again he slaps it off and
resumes.*

MAN. I'm woken by the chip-shop man. His fat face telling me
to, 'Get t'pool, naughty boy! Get to pool!' He sits on my bed
and watches me change into my togs, the dirty fuck! And
we're stood outside the swimming pool. The children from
the village, all twenty of us standing in our togs. And what a
state we are! Like a box of fish fingers with skin all bluey-
white. Little skinny arms wrapped around against cold. I'm
stood next to some fourteen-year-old bloke bursting out of
his trunks. Crikey! Spiky pubic hair, the very look of fills my
belly with jealousy. Look at my own wretched sack. Bald but
for a single hair and sat in my briefs like a tiny canary egg.
Bloody shame! THE SHAME! It's these togs, isn't it?! Togs

that I've been wearing since the age of eight, yes, Mother!
Making my every trip to the swimming pool a torture,
Mother! I'm standing there clamped into these 'baby-blue
panties' and shame shaping out a slug for a prick! Tramp-
tramp-tramp-tramp-tramp-tramp! I see you being marched
up the main street. Your dad marching behind. Your little
brother, he's that covered in brown sauce he looks like he's
shat himself. And he's laughing but we know what's what.

WOMAN. The children huddled together and you make some
apology for your tight trunks and I just smile at you and hold
your hand.

MAN. A surprise then. My one and only gift to you.

WOMAN. What's this?

MAN. I made it for you last night, didn't I.

WOMAN. We can listen to it later in yours.

MAN. Tape recorder shoved against the speaker in the front
room. It's proper good!

WOMAN. What do you mean, 'there mightn't be a later'?

MAN. Are you listening to me?

WOMAN. I take the tape and hide it in my baggy costume.
Keep it safe this lovely tape and hold your hand while we
watch the men and women of the village gather about with
their faces full of the fear and listening to my dad droning on
about spreading the silence even further. Droning on –
droning on – droning on!

MAN. Tick tock tick tock!

WOMAN. Stood in our togs and the chip-shop man hoses us
down all of a sudden. Hands to our faces and we're dropping
to our knees for covered in petrol.

MAN. And that fourteen-year-old boy's dragged out. And what
a little child, all of a sudden he looks like a little girly
standing there. Soaked in petrol and stood in front of his
mum and dad with his little girly cries! The boss man's
words and telling his parents to take their tongues.

WOMAN. I watch my father holding the lighter I bought him for Christmas. I'm watching the boy's mam and dad take each other's tongues with knives and the boy saved.

MAN. It's all busy now with men and women trying to save their children. My mother stood beside the chip-shop man. Knives passed quickly and tongues cut out. Blood and all is bits with words giving over to tears and silence. I'm being dragged inside and I can see you hiding by your mother's side. You're gone from me. You're gone. A breath, a pause…

His clock sounds and he watches it for some time, exhausted. He slowly presses it off. He takes a breath. Slower then.

Inside the swimming pool it's screaming just like the outside. Tongues are being taken just like the grown-ups were. Little children covered in blood tossed into swimming pool. I'm looking at your little brother in his inflatable tortoise. He's bobbing up and down covered in blood and looking dead. Boss man tells me I'll be saved. His work has been done here. It's time to spread the good news from village to village.

He looks at his clock.

Look how these seconds are bullying me. Switching me on and off for fun.

He turns it over on his lap to hide the face.

Finished. I'm finished.

WOMAN. What reason the telling, hey? What purpose all this detail?

She stares at the clock and mouths the seconds until it is her time to continue.

I'm hid under my mother's coat. We're sat on the ground at the edge of the woods with all the other women. All of them made silent and one at a time taken to the woods. I'm seen by a man made silent some six years ago. I seen him around village with his clipboard and stopwatch bringing 'a proper order' to all things. He drags me away from Mother and into woods. I want to bite through my tongue and be done with it all. Shot bodies of old women thrown about the dead wood. Still in my baggy swimsuit and my feet pinching on something or other. He opens my mouth... holds out my tongue with his knife. Close my eyes. I feel him inside my mouth and feel him drag at my hair. Face pressed to ground and punching and fucking in equal measures, you know that sad scene.

Slight pause. Starts to laugh a little.

Turn my head and a deep daydream!

Slight pause.

I'm falling slowly through clouds. It's a good feeling and each cloud softer than next, passing me from one to other, you know. Like a breath on me almost. The clouds soft on my skin, I fall. And then through clouds and into blue and towards the world. And winds light they pass me from one to other like a feather I am. And I fall slow. And I look at the world as it comes to me and me to it. And I see the different greens of our valley, lovely shape of the countryside. Even from here I can see our little village and see the church and woods. I fall. Then into woods and slowly through leaves of beech trees and passed then quietly from branch to branch and arms take me and then I see that it's you. And we fall onto that mattress you made from leaves and I fold into lovely you and we speak. I speak to you, sweetheart.

Slight pause.

Like I'm speaking to you now.

Slight pause.

I can see his gun by my side.

She looks at the clock and smiles a little.

That song then.

She presses the tape recorder and we hear the voice of the MAN *when he was a twelve-year-old* BOY.

BOY. Here's a song. Let's try and learn these words, hey? I'll hold it near speaker.

The song plays. It's The Mills Brothers singing the comedy classic 'Nagasaki'. He can be heard trying to sing along with it. The words come very fast which gets him laughing.

She listens and occasionally tries to mouth some lyrics.

The lyrics sung:

Hot gingerbread and dynamite,
That's all there is at night,
Back in Nagasaki where the fellows chew tobaccky
And the women wicky-wacky-woo!

They got the ways that they entertain,
Would hurry a hurricane.
Back in Nagasaki where the fellows chew tobaccky
And the women wicky-wacky-woo!

In Fujiama, ya get a mama,
Then your troubles increase, boy!
In South Dakota you want a soda,
Hershy-Kershy ten cents piece.

They hug you and kiss you each night,
By jingo, boys, worth that price!
Back in Nagasaki where the fellows chew tobaccky
And the women wicky-wacky-woo!

At exactly 1 minute 41 seconds it comes to an abrupt end. She stops the tape and begins to rewind it.

MAN. Suddenly can't stop thinking of a cup of tea. Not tempting me or nothing but a happy brew. Soak my brittle scheming insides and send me back to the land of the living.

A pause. Grave suddenly.

I remember my last cup.

The tape stops and she kisses the recorder. She stands up.

Will you listen to me?

She goes to the window.

It was maybe a couple of weeks ago now and I'm in the kitchen and once again I'm chatting to you, hey. The kettle boiled and I wrap my hands around cup and remember the softness of your hand when I passed you that tape that last day... you held my hand, remember? I'm telling you this and walking towards the window to look out on the outside and up at that house on the mountain. No warning, really. So I'm a little surprised when I look out window and it's like the empty outside has jumped down my throat. Don't even hear the tea hit the floor – cup smash. Try talking to you but maybe you're not listening to me any more. Look across at that house for a little hope. But I'm too shook. 'Cause I'm standing there and looking down at what were villages, staring at what was life and that road I help build. And here I am with my future... me forever shuffling about with these children's shoes on, the room forever my country, little tracks scratched into this floor showing off my daily routine, my yearly routine, my life's routine. Well, I'm away from the window fast and turn this chair and face against this wall as I am now. Got this empty body whispering about that terrible bad thing that I did, and it's my time!

Slight pause.

Can I allow our words to drown and die like that... like me, with me? Either way the words and I are fucked and the fight is lost and that road and sea waits for me. It's not a question of can I stop talking to you, love... I must give in.

The WOMAN *stands again looking out the window. The light darkening outside.*

WOMAN. Best turn that frown to upside down.

Slight pause.

You allow Mister Misery through our door and I'll be dusting 'til Christmas... whenever that may be.

MAN. Can I leave you alone and just give in?

Long pause as they do very little.

Again these children's shoes pinching me. They know of their arrival soon. Mocking me daily, the bastards!

WOMAN. For years I've passed the very same day just for moments like these. Today feeling different, though. I need to know you're listening to me still.

She turns from the window. She's been crying.

Are you?

Slight pause.

MAN. Yes.

WOMAN. Let me finish to this point! Deep breath, I'll reach the end and find some strength for another day.

She walks back to sit down in her armchair next to him. They both hold their alarm clocks.

They turn to each other and for the very first time their eyes meet.

MAN. Continue for the final time then. Begin.

The timpani drum begins to sound. The drum roll builds in volume and suddenly cuts.

Looking at her clock she resumes.

WOMAN. The ground all loose underneath and deeper into woods I run. Drop his gun and by the river I run. To where? To what plan? Can still taste that fucker in my mouth so spit out. Still soreness all about, so quicken my speed. What thoughts? No thoughts. Run 'til I can't run no more. And night to day and back to night. And a shell of me I am. No tears yet. No fear even. No feelings of fear. Just this running. No feelings of being alive. The daylight merely switching me on and off for fun. And night to day and back to night. And night to day and back to night. My sharp breath, my heart thumping, my legs chewing up soil. Through forest and moorland and steep hills now flat to my speed. Through meadows and farm and wind from the fells no match for me, I run. For days I run. My breath.

She pants for a few seconds and stops.

The rhythm of the run offering me thoughts that come in
pictures and each one is your sweet face and me being pulled
away from you. Each picture of you and I lose you a little
more. Each yard away is yard away from you. And I stop
with days of running behind. I'm stood in heather and
bilberry, my legs all jelly, my face raw from wind and I'm
trying to imagine you by my side. I'm trying to place your
kiss how it used to be, try to hear your voice, try to
remember our words but the wind unkind it blows sweet
remembered words to where ever words float to. Kiss your
tape then! This tape! A little bit of you kept safe! You're
gone from me and for the first time I say those words, 'Are
you listening? Are you listening to me?'

His clock sounds and he slams it off.

MAN. Four boys taken out from the swimming pool with our
voices saved. For what reason are we saved? Outside the
pool and all is men made dumb. They carry out the man you
shot his balls and he wasn't too happy when they fell out the
end of his trousers. The boss man stood up on a car and
shouting his big talk. 'What great clarity this silence! Men
giving over to simple routines and finding a function for
once. Nature given an order.' He starts talking about a new
order. A road that we must build. 'A road for the Silent. A
road that will cut through the countryside and carry us lucky
ones to Paradise.' And we march away with the village
behind left all bloody and empty. March with other villages
in our sights. And night to day and back to night. And night
to day and back to night. Days turn to weeks and little
villages torn up and other people made silent but for what
reason do I still have my voice? The Silent grow. The road
the road the road the road! And set to work. The road a
constant. No pause for night even. And what freedom the
road gives to my body. Shot to life I am. Is this my
moment?! The great engineer! My life given a reason by this
road. Now that you're gone from me a direction through this
great road I build, my back stronger, arms shovelling the
road faster than the other children. Legs marking out my new
future with each step. And it's me in front of the others

shouting just like the boss man does. My face no longer all frightened, fuck no! Now the little lapdog I am. The shifty little grin to the chip-shop man. Kneel in front, take his hand and kiss his pudgy hand. And is that a kindly pat on my head? The boss man dresses me up so that I'm stood apart from the dumb. The road flattening the green, and with each yard travelled it's more him I am than me. Again! It's more him I am than me!

WOMAN. The walk takes me its own course. Funny little legs led by the what-ifs. Driven slower but no less easier. No respite even. I'm looking for what? No answers. No questions to start. Just this aimless walking. I'm a child. Our village long gone, I rest in some wood. What was your face? Is it months? Is it really months past since? Heart more numbed than heavy. A breath for fear I'll blow up. A breath a pause a breath.

A pause.

The noise of a road being built in the distance behind. A little boy running scared from his village. Tells me about the men with knives who've come to bring silence and spread routine. The road they're building towards Paradise. Visions of my dad sitting at the breakfast table counting out those cornflakes making that orange square.

A pause.

I ask the boy to speak of other things and he does. I close my eyes and listen to those words returned. I tell him to make the small talk and just listen to the ebb and flow of those smaller words as he talks of the small things. And I talk too and our words entwine and with each word passed our old world is rebuilt somehow. The woods a bubble it keeps this hidden world safe and away from that road being built. And eyes still closed I take his face and I kiss him.

Slight pause.

I look at his shiny black shoes and red laces. Despite it all, a hope found in these funny little shoes.

Slight pause.

A boy calls his name.

His delivery slower too.

MAN. The road stopped by some woods. I enter with the boss man. 'A naughty boy ran off from that last village and he needs catching.' The boss man behind and I search the boy out. I call his name. I know now why my tongue has been saved. I call out for the boy and soon he comes running out towards me. He's all talk of another child that's nearby who needs saving too… a little girl he jabbers on about. I'm using my words to calm him. I'm using my words to lie to him. All the time I can see the boss man through the trees with his eyes on us. The kitchen knife he placed in my hand and to cut to the silence I push it far into the boy's mouth. I can't look at his face and stare down at his little black shoes and red laces.

A pause.

The boss man makes me put them on. 'Shoes fit for a Judas.' (*Breaking*.) And I am.

A pause. Outside is growing darker.

And run run run RUN RUN RUN RUN RUN RUN RUN!

WOMAN. And so begins my final run and where to this run? The screams of that boy in the distance and again the woods they take me and me through them.

MAN. And the woods through me I run away from that boy, away from that road. I run and through the woods.

WOMAN. And the woods no more and only this mountain to climb.

MAN. And higher I climb with that boy's face at every turn, with silence below and the road leading into the sea. The land emptying of the Silent with the boss man watching and guiding, guiding and watching as the Silent walk into the sea, their Paradise. I climb. And surely there's safety in the skies. And your face it guides me upwards. It takes me to where's safe.

WOMAN. And your face it guides me upwards and finds me this house and keeps me safe. It comforts me and opens my day and closes my night.

MAN. Inside this house and I lose myself in our past.

WOMAN. And I speak to you daily though you are not here and surely in the sea.

MAN. And speak to you daily though you are surely dead, love. Life passes and memory repeats.

WOMAN. Sat at table and mixing the meringues and looking at Mother at sink.

MAN. The parquet floor and my little heart all a flutter and Mother's breasts.

WOMAN. And the shape of town and speckled light and the gentle seasons passing.

MAN. And Mother's quilt and the smell of her bedroom and my face lost in that bra.

WOMAN. And the picture of the younger you standing at the cake table.

MAN. And bobbing about in my underpants talking like Auntie Ada. And the younger you. The lovely you and the river sounds and the stillness of us.

WOMAN. And your arms about me and sleep and your warm breath on my back.

MAN. And our mattress made from leaves.

WOMAN. And our mattress made from leaves.

MAN. Are you listening to me?

WOMAN. And are you listening to me?

MAN. Am I the last to talk?

WOMAN. 'Cause surely I'm the last.

MAN. Can I leave the words and find a proper sleep?

WOMAN. I am the last and yet the words much bigger than me. For words they float.

MAN. Us up in the skies spelt out in the small words and joined for ever.

Long pause. They are still and silent.

WOMAN. I am alone here in this house though never quite alone. I pause. I feel fear. It subsides. The words trap and yet keep me. They float upwards and find their way as I find mine. Are you still speaking? Can I sleep?

A pause.

MAN. My insides are still now and wait. The outside silent, the world that was there not a stir, that house on that mountain and my house here, the cupboard without tea, the children's shoes, the road, the cold sea and Paradisc... life and death paused then and wait for my choice.

A pause.

So what purpose my telling and what purpose me?

A pause.

To speak. (*Whispers to himself.*) To speak.

A pause. He smiles a little.

WOMAN. I can sleep then.

She closes her eyes and she vanishes from the space.

He is suddenly alone on the stage.

Long pause.

MAN. I'm alone here in my house... though never alone, hey love? I'll sleep and in the morning, as always, I'll continue... and I *will* speak... and we will live a life.

A pause.

Yes.

He closes his eyes as the timpani drum is faded up loud and the red-velvet curtains slowly close.

Blackout.

The End.

LYNNDIE'S GOTTA GUN

A play for former US soldier Private Lynndie England

Lynndie's Gotta Gun was first performed by Artistas Unidos at Teatro Nacional D. Maria II, Lisbon, on 16 June 2005, as part of the Conferência de Imprensa e Outras Aldrabices, a collection of sketches inspired by Harold Pinter. The cast was as follows:

MAN   Gonçalo Waddingtin
LYNNDIE   Joana Bárcia

Director   Jorge Silva Melo
Designer   Rita Lopes Alves and João Calvário
Lighting Designer Pedro Domingos

Characters

MAN

LYNNDIE

BOY, *non-speaking*

Lights up.

A MAN *stands on stage looking into the wings.*

He is out of breath and looks terrified.

A children's party clown, LYNNDIE, *walks fast on the stage carrying a large fish.*

She smashes the MAN *on the face with the fish.*

The MAN *falls to the ground.*

A pause.

MAN. I don't understand what I'm doing here.

   LYNNDIE *slaps him on the head with the fish.*

   She turns and leaves.

   The MAN *gets to his feet.*

   LYNNDIE *re-enters carrying a very large frying pan.*

   She smacks the MAN *hard across the head.*

   Again he hits the ground fast.

   She stands over him.

   What have you done with my son? I came in with my son but I haven't seen him? I heard a gunshot!

   LYNNDIE *turns and walks offstage.*

   As the MAN *gets to his feet* LYNNDIE *re-enters carrying a large cream cake.*

   She fires it into the MAN*'s face.*

   Long pause as she looks at him.

LYNNDIE. Tell me what you know.

MAN. I don't know anything.

LYNNDIE. You're lying.

MAN. I promise you I'm not.

LYNNDIE. We've been trained to deal with liars. You're lying.

MAN. I'm not lying.

LYNNDIE. You know things.

MAN. What sort of things?

LYNNDIE. Things we need to know. Information.

MAN. I don't have any information.

LYNNDIE. Every man has information.

MAN. Yes, of course.

LYNNDIE. So you're no different.

MAN. Yes but I'm sure I don't have *specific* information. The information you want.

LYNNDIE. How would you know that?

MAN. Well, why don't you tell me what information you want to hear and I can tell you whether I know it or not.

LYNNDIE. Well, that would be Classified. Are you trying to get me in trouble with my superior?

MAN. What are you talking about?

LYNNDIE. Are you a difficult man?

MAN. No.

LYNNDIE. Would your wife say that you're a difficult man?

MAN. My wife?!

LYNNDIE. You have a son. Do you have a wife?

MAN. I did have a wife but she was taken away.

LYNNDIE. Why was she taken?

MAN. The same reason you took me.

LYNNDIE. Which is?

MAN. You thought she had information, I suppose.

LYNNDIE. Answer my question. Are you a difficult man?

MAN. Not especially. Look, I heard a gun shot!

LYNNDIE. Then you're just playing a part. Usually you're a
nice guy but today you're being a fucking cunt – excuse my
language.

MAN. How long will I be kept here?

LYNNDIE. Have I been polite to you?!

MAN. Can I talk to your superior...

LYNNDIE. I'm nice. I don't want to torture you but you're
beginning to push buttons, do you understand? Now you can
tell me what you know or I can start torturing you. You decide.

MAN. Well, what sort of things do you want to hear?

LYNNDIE. Do you like us?

MAN. Do I *like* you?

LYNNDIE. It's the important question.

MAN. Is it?

LYNNDIE. If you like us I don't have a problem with you, do I?

MAN. I suppose not.

LYNNDIE. Well, don't you think I'm nice? Don't you think I'm
a funny person?

MAN. Are you serious?

LYNNDIE. Oh, I'm deadly serious. Am I your friend, Brad?!

MAN. My name isn't Brad.

LYNNDIE. Let me call you Brad, it's easier. You call me
Lynndie. Am I your friend, Brad?

MAN. I don't know you, Lynndie. I've never met you before.

LYNNDIE. Am I *funny*, though? Am I good to have around? Do you think we can work things out, Brad? Our differences. Will we always have these little differences between us? You and me. Me and you. You're not answering me, Brad!

MAN. Well, what do you want me to say?! You want me to say that you are my friend.

LYNNDIE *turns and exits. She re-enters holding a black pistol. She points it at the* MAN.

I'm sorry. I've obviously hurt your feelings.

LYNNDIE. It's not you especially. They've trained me in negotiating but it's tiring, isn't it? I'm not very good at it and I'm angry about that.

MAN. Please, Lynndie, try to negotiate some more.

LYNNDIE. I'm not even sure what we're negotiating any more. I've travelled a long way and to be honest I really hoped for a better relationship with you people. I had it in my mind what it might be. A relationship with someone like you who doesn't know my background. I had this strange idea that maybe we might be friends… because I'm a friendly girl, you see. I could take you back with me and you could be my foreign boyfriend. I had this idea that maybe we'd get married and that friends would always ask us how we got married. We're at Thanksgiving and we're telling the story of how we met in this terrible place. How we connected despite our culture. The President would send us a telegram and congratulate us on our union. Our photograph would be printed on a calendar of how things *really* are and what great love freedom brings. (*Slight pause.*) It hasn't worked out like that, has it, Brad?

MAN. Is that the gun you used on my son?

LYNNDIE. You people are so ungrateful. I've tried to be nice, haven't I?

MAN. Tell me you didn't shoot him?

A pause.

LYNNDIE. Tell me you like me first.

A pause.

MAN. I like you.

LYNNDIE. 'I really like you, Lynndie.'

A pause.

MAN. I really like you, Lynndie.

LYNNDIE. You see now we're talking, Brad. We're putting aside our differences and you're getting to know me more. This is the way things work in a civilised country.

MAN. Now tell me you didn't shoot my son, please.

LYNNDIE. Oh, why are you asking that, Brad?

MAN. Because I need to know!

LYNNDIE. Just when we were getting all friendly you had to hurt my feelings!

MAN. Please tell me!

LYNNDIE. You've just got no idea of the sacrifices we're making, FUCKER!

LYNNDIE *fires her pistol and a little flag comes out with 'Bang' on it.*

The MAN *laughs from exasperation.*

MAN. He's still alive then. Thank you, Lynndie. That was funny.

Suddenly she pulls out another gun and shoots him dead.

She stands over his body and watches the blood appear around him.

She takes off her red nose and places it on his face.

A ten-year-old BOY *walks onstage.*

He stops and looks over at her.

She faces him.

LYNNDIE *reloads her gun and points it at the* BOY.

Blackout.

The End.

CHATROOM

Chatroom was originally performed as part of the 2005 NT Connections season. It received its first professional production in the Cottesloe auditorium of the National Theatre, London, on 10 March 2006. The cast was as follows:

WILLIAM	Matt Smith
JACK	Javone Prince
EVA	Matti Houghton
EMILY	Andrea Riseborough
JIM	Andrew Garfield
LAURA	Naomi Bentley

Director	Anna Mackmin
Designer	Jonathan Fensom
Lighting Designer	Jason Taylor
Sound Designer	Christopher Shutt
Video Designer	Dick Straker
Music	Paddy Cunneen

Characters

WILLIAM

JACK

EVA

EMILY

JIM

LAURA

There are six identical orange plastic seats in a row at the very front of the stage. There's a two-metre gap between each seat.

'Oompa Loompa' sung by the Oompa Loompas, from the film Willy Wonka and the Chocolate Factory, *is heard.*

During this song three actors appear from one side of the stage and two others appear from the other side. They walk casually towards each other in a line, stop, turn and face the audience.

From left to right they are WILLIAM, JACK, EVA, EMILY *and* LAURA. *They are all about fifteen/sixteen years of age. They stand there for a while and look at the audience.*

They then look at each other. They seem to be sizing each other up. In unison they walk towards their seats and sit down.

This should all last one and half minutes.

As they sit the Oompa Loompas' song comes to an end.

Lights.

WILLIAM. You're depressing me now.

JACK. Really?

WILLIAM. You see, you've lost me. At the beginning I was with you. But not now. I'm a little disappointed.

JACK. Sorry.

WILLIAM. You really think that? You've thought it over, came to an opinion, you believe that?

JACK. It is popular.

WILLIAM. Well, so is body-piercing but that isn't a good thing, is it?

JACK. I suppose.

WILLIAM. So let's look at the facts. A single man lives in a castle in the middle of... where is it set again?

JACK. Film or book?

WILLIAM. There's a difference?

JACK. Both films changed some details. It doesn't really matter.

WILLIAM. Well, in the book it's set where ever it's set... and this man lives in his big house in the middle of the town. He lives with dwarfs. Nothing wrong with that. But they're orange. Orange dwarfs with green hair.

JACK. And there's only twenty of them making the world's supply of chocolate... none of this is meant to be realistic.

WILLIAM. But why make them dwarfs? Why the green hair? Why make them orange in the first place?! Can you see where I'm going with this?

JACK. Kind of.

WILLIAM. What's wrong with the ordinary?

JACK. It's for children. Ordinary's boring, maybe?

WILLIAM. Which is my original point about these children's writers! As if a little boy who shares a giant bed with his grandparents... four of them! As if he'd ever in the real world win this extraordinary chocolate empire!

JACK (*groans*). Yeah.

WILLIAM. You know in the real world it would have been that fat German boy who falls into the chocolate lake at the beginning of the tour. In the real world he's the winner.

JACK. I think I might have to...

WILLIAM. This is how it really ends. He falls in. His father gets these big-time lawyers to sue the shit out of Willy Wonka. They look into his shady past, his very dodgy personal life with those orange midgets. He's dragged through the tabloids with paedophilia ringing in his ears. They make shit out of him! Willy Wonka is no more. He's done. He's doing twenty-five years in a high-security prison being passed around his fellow prisoners like the proverbial box of Quality Street. In the outside, the Germans win, 'cause let's face it, the Germans always win. The fat German kiddie...

JACK. His name is Augustus.

WILLIAM. Right, Augustus... well, he inherits everything as part of his settlement. He gets it all. And because he's a fat glutton he can't stop eating all this chocolate. The more the Oompa Loompas make, the more Augustus eats. He's eighteen years old and forty stone. One day he wakes up, stretches for the television remote and dies of a massive coronary sclerosis. That is the real world. Do you understand this? Where exactly are you getting confused?

JACK. It's only a children's story.

WILLIAM. It's a lie! What's the point? What are they telling us?

JACK. What are who telling us?

WILLIAM. The writers! Our parents! Harry fucking Potter!?! In the real world he's still under the stairs. He's a thirty-year-old retard who's developed his own under-the-stairs language!

JACK. The point is...

WILLIAM. Yes?!

JACK. The point is... is that children don't want to read the true stories. What child wants to read the news?! It's just escape. It's important that we dream of other things.

WILLIAM. Fuck off! Life's too short. If the world is going to evolve in any way... children should be told what's really happening. Cold, clear facts... that's what's taken us down from the trees, that's what powers economy...

JACK. A lot of these children's stories are metaphors. The writers are expressing important issues in creative ways!

WILLIAM. 'Expressing important'…?! You see, you're depressing me again!

JACK (*to himself*). Fuck's sake.

WILLIAM. Do you think any eight-year-old finishing reading *Charlie and the Chocolate Factory* thinks anything other than, 'I'd love a Never-ending Gobstopper, Grandpa!'?! Listen to me, John…

JACK. It's Jack.

WILLIAM. They're trying to keep children young! Adults. Publishers. Fucking writers. They don't want children thinking for themselves. They see children as a threat. They want to keep everything 'fantasy'. This J.K. Rowling woman! She is the enemy. She should be taken out. Erased. Removed. Exterminated.

A pause.

JACK. So that's what you're doing in a Harry Potter Chatroom? Trying to drum up some interest in an assassination attempt on J.K. Rowling?

A slight pause.

WILLIAM. Well, are you interested?

A slight pause.

JACK. I can't. I have to do my geography homework.

Lights.

EVA. But I was younger then and she just came on the scene, remember?

EMILY. Yeah.

EVA. You're ten years of age and that's a critical age. You're starting to feel uncomfortable in your childishness, aren't you?

EMILY. It's the hormones.

EVA. And the video with her at school in her school uniform and pigtails...

EMILY. She looked lovely.

EVA. You wanted to be her, didn't ya?

EMILY. She didn't have her tits done then?

EVA. That was much later.

EMILY. But even then they were a decent size. Certainly a B-cup.

EVA. But at ten you wanted to be her. And that video... wasn't it a bit creepy... in hindsight... but that thing she was doing with her tongue. It was very sexual.

EMILY. We didn't notice.

EVA. We were young and it wasn't for the kiddies.

EMILY. It was for the older boys and the daddies.

EVA. She's in her school uniform with her pigtails and sticking out her tongue but it's subtle. Flicking it in and out like a little parrot.

EMILY. It was a bit seedy.

EVA. So I'm watching that video after not seeing it since I was ten... and I have to say I felt betrayed by Britney. You know how her songs and videos were all about that journey from girl to woman...

EMILY. Yeah.

EVA. And it sort of felt good, didn't it? Like Britney Spears was a part of your puberty.

EMILY. I remember having my first period and listening to 'I'm Not a Girl, Not Yet a Woman' and thinking, 'Thanks Britney. My sentiments exactly!'

EVA. She felt like a spokeswoman.

EMILY. Oh, definitely.

EVA. But as I watched 'Hit Me Baby One More Time' and all that sexual stuff with her tongue and just how cropped that crop-top was…

EMILY. Was her belly button pierced back then?

EVA. Probably.

EMILY. Sorry go on.

EVA. I got really angry over that betrayal. It's no longer Britney who's talking to us but some pervert record producer. He's got this vision, this plan of turning every ten-year-old girl in the Western world into a tongue-flicking, crop-topped, belly-button-pierced temptress.

EMILY. Have you got your belly button pierced?

EVA. Yeah, of course.

EMILY. Did it hurt?

EVA. It's not as bad as you hear. But anyway Britney, Britney…!

EMILY. Yeah, Britney.

EVA. Don't you think a lot of young girls began to feel that betrayal?

EMILY. It's possible. Both of us did.

EVA. And maybe that's why her career died a slow death. She lied to us.

EMILY. You don't think it has to do with her music being shit?

EVA. A little bit… but I really would like to think that girls realised that they were being manipulated… that they made a stand against that pervert record producer… but do you know what the sad thing is?

EMILY. Britney got burnt.

EVA. She was thick.

EMILY. She made her money, I suppose.

EVA. She lost our respect. She's got a few houses, nice clothes, new breasts… but if I met her tomorrow…

EMILY. Like on the bus?

EVA. Or in Tesco.

EMILY. Or Topshop!

EVA. Or Argos.

EMILY. Debenhams, maybe!

EVA. If I met Britney Spears tomorrow I would gently pull her to one side, place my arms around her shoulders like I'm going to hug her, move my face towards her like I'm going to kiss her… and whisper in her ear, 'Britney Spears, you sold my childhood soul.'

EMILY. Oh, that's cruel.

EVA. 'You sold my childhood soul.' Then I'd smash her in the face.

EMILY. And what would Britney say?

EVA. 'Hit me baby one more time.'

EMILY. Of course.

EVA. Her day of judgement will come when some teenage girl will stop her outside Prada and say, 'You sold my childhood soul, bitch.'

EMILY *laughs but* EVA *doesn't. She's serious.*

A pause.

EMILY. I better go. It's been very nice talking to you, whoever you are.

EVA. Can we talk some more? I had an argument with my bitch-mother and I'm feeling terrible.

EMILY. Okay. (*Pause.*) So what do you want to talk about?

A pause. EVA *thinks and decides.*

EVA. Murder.

Music.

JIM (*fifteen*) *walks on stage and stops. He faces the audience and sighs. He walks to his seat next to* LAURA *and sits.*

Music cuts.

Lights.

JIM. And you really don't mind listening to this?

LAURA. That's what the room's all about.

JIM. But you'd say if you did mind? If it was too draining, too annoying, too boring maybe...?

LAURA. I don't mind listening.

A pause.

JIM. Maybe I shouldn't be even in this place. I don't know whether it's that serious yet.

LAURA (*direct*). There isn't a scale of depression here. I'm here at the other end and I'm here to listen to you. If you want to talk, Jim, then talk. If you don't, then don't talk.

A pause.

JIM. Right.

LAURA. Don't be nervous.

JIM. I'll talk then.

LAURA. Okay.

A pause.

JIM. I'm a Roman Catholic... and it's last Easter... and ahhh... and every year our parish does a big Passion play in our local church. My mother's very active in the church. She's the Virgin Mary.

LAURA. Which would make you Jesus Christ.

JIM. In the Passion play she's the Virgin Mary.

LAURA. I understand.

JIM. And my whole family get involved. I've got three older brothers and they're Roman soldiers. They're very broad… not like me… and they look the part. One year my brother Derek went too heavy on Jesus and actually popped his knee right open. It was a mess. But anyway, this year and my mother runs into my bedroom with her 'terrific news'. She's building it up like she's going to tell me that I'm going to get a stab at playing a centurion… until she tells me… they want me to play John.

LAURA. Well, John's a great part.

JIM. Yeah, but he's a bit gay.

LAURA. How do you mean?

JIM. I've got nothing against gay people.

LAURA. St John was gay?

JIM. Historically speaking, he probably wasn't gay. But in our parish it's always the slightly effeminate boys who get to play John.

LAURA. Okay.

JIM. Like I say… I've got nothing against gays. I respect the gay community. They're tough, they know their own mind, they stand out and they don't care, you know. I respect them. But I'm not like that at all. I'm just a sap with no bottle who knows nothing. I'm not interesting enough to play the gay icon that is St John. In a million years I could never get away with those lime robes.

LAURA. Lime?

JIM. It's sort of an unspoken thing in the parish. It's a bit weird.

LAURA. Right, carry on.

JIM. We do a few rehearsals with my mother as the Virgin Mary and I've got to get emotional when Jesus is dying on the cross and he says to Mary, 'Woman, behold your son,' while looking over at me. And I'm supposed to break down at that point because I know that Jesus is just about to croak it but I'm getting very nervous because basically I'm a terrible actor and I'm all blocked up.

LAURA. Emotionally blocked?

JIM. Exactly.

LAURA. Right.

JIM. So I tell my mother I want to drop out of the play. I say it quiet so the others can't hear but she starts screaming at me and saying how typical it was... and did I have a backbone?... and why was I such a coward?... and why wasn't I like my older brothers... and all this shit. And then she says I'm like my dad. But what would I know?... I haven't seen my dad since I was six... but she starts shouting, 'You're just like your dad, Jim!... Just like your dad, walking out on things! Walking out on me! Gutless!' I mean, I hate her just then. Why did she have to bring up my dad in front of all of those people like that. Why?! So the following night is the Passion play proper and I'm kneeling and looking up at Jesus. He's doing a wonderful job dying on the cross, this guy called Nick Lawson. He's into amateur dramatics in a big way... I actually saw him in a production of *Babes in the Wood* playing the Widow Twankey and I swear to God he was hilarious... but as Jesus Christ he was even better... obviously not in a hilarious way but...

LAURA. I understand.

JIM. Right. So Nick's line to me and my mother is coming up and I'm still really furious with her from the night before. 'Woman, behold your son,' cries Nick. (*Pause.*) At the start I didn't know whether it was his great delivery or just thinking about my mother being my mother... but I started to cry. I'm crying really hard. People are thinking that this is wonderful.

I completely upstage Nick's crucifixion and the night's suddenly about St John and whether he's going to be all right and if he'll have the strength to carry on and start and finish his gospel. But anyway! Anyway! Afterwards and my mother is having a lemonade in the sacristy and I'm out of my lime robes and looking over at her. And I realise why I was crying back then. (*Pause*.) I was crying because I know my mother doesn't like me. (*Pause*.) If I really remind her of the man she hates, the man who left us when I was six... then maybe I should walk away too. But where to? Where do I go to?

A pause.

LAURA. The rule in the room is we don't give advice. We just listen.

JIM. Okay.

A pause.

So what about you? Do you have anything you want to share?

LAURA. I just listen.

JIM. No problems?

LAURA. Of course... but I prefer to listen to other people's.

JIM. What do you get out of that?

LAURA. I'm not too sure.

Slight pause.

JIM. Knowing that there are other teenagers struggling probably makes you feel better about your own problems.

LAURA. No.

A pause.

JIM. These are very strange places, aren't they? Like I said, I don't know whether I should be really here. Whether it's that serious yet. What do you think?

LAURA. As I said…

JIM. 'The rule in the room is we don't give advice.' Fine. (*He sighs. Pause.*) Have you been to many suicide chatrooms?

LAURA. Yes.

JIM. And do they help you?

LAURA. Who said I needed to be helped?

A pause.

JIM. Can I know your real name?

LAURA. You can call me Laura.

JIM. But is that your real name?

LAURA. Maybe.

JIM. What city are you from?

LAURA. It doesn't matter. None of that really matters. You just need to know that there's someone listening to you. That's enough, isn't it?

JIM. I suppose.

A pause.

Will we talk about something else, Laura?

LAURA. I don't talk, I listen. You talk.

JIM. Talk about what?

A pause.

LAURA. Tell me about the day your father went missing.

Lights.

Music for some time. We watch them do nothing.

Music cuts abruptly.

Lights.

WILLIAM. We need to set rules.

EMILY. Why?

EVA. We don't use our real names. We don't say what schools we're from…

WILLIAM. We know we're from the same area and that's enough. Just leave out the details. It gives us more freedom.

EVA. Keeps it impersonal.

WILLIAM. I'll use William.

EVA. I'll be Eva.

JACK. I always use Jack.

EMILY. Emily.

EVA. How do we know you're not two middle-aged men trying to get off chatting up two teenage girls?

WILLIAM. How do we know you're not two frustrated housewives trying to take advantage of two innocent altar boys?

EMILY. Are you altar boys?

JACK. Are you desperate housewives?

EMILY / EVA / WILLIAM / JACK. No.

WILLIAM. Excellent.

JACK. I was an altar boy.

WILLIAM. Oh, fuck.

JACK. No, I quite liked it.

EVA. How?

JACK. When you're seven you've got a very simple idea of life and for a while, dressed in my altar boy's gown every Sunday, I really thought I was some sort of angel. I called myself 'an angel-waiter'.

EMILY. 'Angel-waiter'?

JACK. You see, I believed in Adam and Eve and that God created everything in six days and that he had a rest on the Sunday. And I had this image of the church being like a restaurant/café for God to rest in...

EVA. Or a McDonald's?

JACK. Exactly. And it was my job as an angel-waiter to serve him on his day off.

EVA. So what does God eat?

WILLIAM. Chicken nuggets.

EMILY *laughs*.

JACK. I was only seven.

EMILY. That's very cute.

EVA. How long did you think this?

JACK. Several months.

EMILY. And the whole altar-boy thing?

JACK. Four years.

EVA. Four years?!

EMILY. Are you religious now?

WILLIAM. I'd rather not talk about religion? You either do or you don't believe. End of discussion.

EVA (*to herself*). Dick.

WILLIAM. We're all around fifteen, sixteen. We're all middle-class kids of varying wealth growing up in and around Chiswick. I think we know each other's views on boring issues like religion.

EMILY. Oh, right. So what's mine?

WILLIAM (*quickly*). You're disillusioned with the official Church and yet you remain spiritual and have defined your own personal religion based upon the simple idea... that people should be nice to each other.

Slight pause.

EMILY. Bastard.

EVA *laughs.*

WILLIAM. It's a cliché. We're all clichés...

JACK. Yeah, all people can be placed in little boxes like that.

WILLIAM. They can.

EVA. So what are you?

WILLIAM. A pain in the arse.

EVA. Apart from that.

WILLIAM. I'm a cynic. I'm an angry cynic.

EVA. Very attractive.

WILLIAM. I'm not interested in being attractive. Why should I be?

EVA. Because attractive people go further...

WILLIAM. Yeah, I think I glanced at that article in one of my sister's magazines...

EVA. People see a cynic as a black hole. They're nothing. While a person who might be attractive or charming... well, they're at the very centre of things... changing things... manipulating events. What are you but a bad smell.

WILLIAM. That's very kind of you.

EVA. You know what I mean.

WILLIAM. You think I'm heavy-handed?

EMILY. You certainly sound that way.

JACK. He's bloody opinionated.

WILLIAM. Well, that's the name of this room, isn't it!? 'Chiswick's Bloody Opinionated'!

EMILY (*groans*). Christ.

WILLIAM. I'm at the age… we're all at the age when we have to stand up for something. To me it's not about making friends and going bowling and sitting in McDonald's bumming cigarettes and talking about the latest McFly LP… that's a waste of fucking time! Now's the time to be a pain in the arse and step away from other people. We're teenagers! That used to mean something. It was about revolution. Apart from the punks, what have teenagers achieved in the last thirty years? Nothing.

JACK. Did punks achieve something?

WILLIAM. They made their mark! They were angry and they showed it.

EMILY. My mother was a punk. We've got this photograph from 1979 and she's got a cold sore on her cheek the size of a tennis ball. Quite amazing.

EVA. It was dirty work being a punk.

WILLIAM. Nowadays teenagers wouldn't go that far before cracking open their cleansers.

EMILY. Oh, definitely.

JACK. I don't know about that. I cultivated a boil on my neck last year for a few weeks. My mother brought me to the doctor and I was gutted when he said he wouldn't lance it…

EVA. Aww…

JACK. But he gave me this black plaster with this tiny hole in the middle. It sort of draws the pus out towards the little hole.

EVA. Do we have…

JACK. So I'm watching television with my dad and my baby brother and above the telly I hear this noise. (*Makes a quiet splurting noise.*) I swear to God it hit the wall behind me.

EMILY. That's disgusting.

JACK. But it was a revolution!

EVA. How?

JACK. My body was revolting.

EVA (*slow*). Oh, the comedy.

WILLIAM. But does anyone know what I'm talking about?

EMILY. Not really.

EVA. Yeah, I do.

WILLIAM. Finally!

EVA. I went on an anti-war march and for an hour or so I felt really good and I felt empowered. But it was just so small. In the great big scheme of my life it was just one hour of saying that I believed in something.

EMILY. Oh, yeah.

WILLIAM (*to himself*). Oh, please.

EVA. I suppose the rest of the time we're sleepwalking and waiting for something to happen instead of making something happen. It would be so great to accomplish something important. To have a cause.

JACK. William wants to assassinate J.K. Rowling.

EMILY *and* EVA *laugh*.

WILLIAM. I was only joking.

JACK. You talked about it for an hour last week in the Harry Potter Chatroom.

WILLIAM. It's not her personally... it's the idea of her... what she stands for.

EMILY. And what's that?

JACK. William reckons children's writers simplify everything to keep children simple.

WILLIAM. They see us as a threat.

EVA. Who do?

JACK. Adults.

WILLIAM. It's like the adults support these writers to write these pointless stories of fantasy so that children have this cutesy warped idea of what life is about.

EVA. So J.K. Rowling is the field marshal?

WILLIAM. She's the enemy. Not her but the idea of her. If I could kill the idea of her without getting her hurt, I'd do it tomorrow.

EMILY. Are you actually a lunatic?

WILLIAM. I just want to do something important! It's frustrating.

EVA. Would you ever kill anything, William?

WILLIAM. No. Any idiot can kill something. Where's the glory in that?

JACK. Aren't you meant to say that each life is sacred?

EMILY. Exactly.

EVA. That's crap.

WILLIAM. There are some people and life is just wasted on them. Terrorists, dictators, racists...

JACK. PE teachers.

EMILY *laughs*.

WILLIAM. They don't do anything. They suck all the goodness out of living.

JACK. Like William.

WILLIAM. Shut up.

EVA. I think William just wants a cause. He wants to see that cause through. He wants to make a big statement.

WILLIAM. Yes, exactly. I want to make a big statement. Who doesn't?! (*Slight pause*.) Thanks, Eve.

EVA. It's Eva.

WILLIAM. Right. Eva.

Long pause where the four of them do very little.

Then:

JIM. Is there anyone there?

A light comes up on JIM.

Are people still awake? Is this room really called 'Chiswick's Bloody Opinionated'?

WILLIAM. We don't use our real names, names of schools, any details. It's enough that we know that we come from the same area.

JIM. Right. I'll be Jim, then.

EVA. Hello, Jim, I'm Eva.

EMILY. Emily.

JACK. Jack.

WILLIAM. I'm William.

JIM. So what happens here? I don't know this place. What's up?

WILLIAM. Heated discussion. Chit-chat. Bullshit.

EVA. We're looking for a cause? William wants to make a statement.

JACK. We're all a bit frustrated.

EVA. If you have any causes handy, feel free.

A pause.

JIM. Can we talk about our problems here?

EVA. Oh, God.

A pause. WILLIAM *laughs a little. Then:*

WILLIAM. Have you got problems, Jim?

JIM. Yeah, I do.

EMILY. Are they big problems?

JIM. Well, I think so. Big to me anyway.

WILLIAM. And you want us to listen to these big problems and give you some advice?

JACK. Jesus, William…!

A pause.

JIM. Are you still there? Look, I'll go to another room if you want.

WILLIAM *starts laughing to himself.*

A pause.

WILLIAM. Jim?

A pause.

JIM. Yes?

WILLIAM. We're here to help you.

Lights.

Music. They do very little. Maybe they get up.

Music cuts.

Lights.

JIM. So I've been bullied all the way through primary and now in secondary school. I'm very skinny and a bit funny looking so it goes with the territory. You expect it. But I have bigger worries… deeper worries that I can't really explain. And that's tricky. And very recently I've started to feel, 'What's the point? What's the point in everything!' But not in a moaning, teenagey way…

WILLIAM. Your depression isn't pretension.

JIM. How do you mean?

WILLIAM. You're genuinely depressed.

JIM. One hundred per cent genuine! I'm not one of these people who keeps an altar to Kurt Cobain or anything like that. I actually can't stand Nirvana. I don't need their music to feed my depression. I can happily do it all by myself…

EVA. Obviously not happily.

JIM. Yeah! Yeah, 'happily's' the wrong word… but you know what I mean.

JACK. What does depression feel like?

WILLIAM. It feels great, what do you think!

JACK. No, I know it's crap… I just want to know what it feels like to Jim.

A pause. A look of exasperation on WILLIAM*'s face.*

WILLIAM. Well, Jim?

A pause.

JIM. It's like the whole world has turned into soup. Everything has the consistency of soup. And your insides and your heart… well, they just sort of ache… and it's like you're clogged up with about five sliced loaves of bread. It's exactly like that.

Slight pause.

EMILY. Wow.

JACK. Depression's like bread and soup?

EVA. Shut up, Jack!

JACK. I'm only repeating…

JIM. The food comparison probably doesn't work.

WILLIAM. Schizophrenics often say they feel like a mixed salad.

EVA, JACK *and* WILLIAM *laugh.* JIM *smiles.*

EMILY. You sound sweet. Do you have a girlfriend?

WILLIAM. Ohh, wait a second! We're here to give Jim some advice...

EMILY. I just wanted to know if you had anyone close to you. You don't have anyone in your family to talk to... so I thought maybe an understanding girlfriend would help you to...

WILLIAM. Jesus, Emily, if you'd been listening to Jim for the last hour you wouldn't ask that. Jim doesn't have our normal teenagey problems. It's not a problem that can be solved by a quick feel outside the chip shop!

EVA. He's different.

WILLIAM. Of course he'd love a girlfriend! But that can't happen 'cause he's dealing with just getting up in the morning and facing into another one of his shitty days!

JIM. I'm not that bad...

EVA. Maybe think before you speak, Emily!

EMILY. Piss off!

EVA. No, it's just bullshit! I expected more from you! You didn't strike me as some head-in-the-sand princess.

EMILY. I'm not like that!

WILLIAM. Selfish cow!

EMILY. Jesus, all I said was...

WILLIAM. Jim has the courage to come into this room and open up and tell us all this pathetic crap. All you're asked to do is imagine that others can be different from you.

EMILY. You have no idea what I'm like…

EVA. Well, by a comment like that… like Jim could be cured by the heart of a good girl…

EMILY. I didn't mean…

WILLIAM. Sorry about this, Jim…

JIM. No, really, it's…

EVA. I think we've all got a good impression of the type of girl you are, Emily!

EMILY. Fuck off!

EVA. Living in a little suburban bubble. Small group of girlfriends who hang around after music lessons sniggering over copies of *Bliss*.

WILLIAM. They're all called Sarah, right. Sarah-Jane, Sarah-Marie, Sarah-Louise, Sarah-Anne…

EVA. The hairband brigade in your deck shoes and Lacrosse shirts…

WILLIAM. What's the worst that's happened to you?

JACK. Oh, come on, guys…

WILLIAM. Scuffed your chinos in the park?! That night Daddy didn't pick you up from Pizza Hut and you had to get the bus home!!

EVA. Or maybe when your pony had to be put down 'cause your big fat preppy arse was buckling its back…

JACK. Hoy!

WILLIAM. Shut up, Jack!

EMILY. I had anorexia, you know!

EVA. So what!

WILLIAM. Weekend anorexia, was it?! Bursting out of those chinos?! Had to shift a few pounds?

EMILY (*to herself*). What?

EVA. Anorexia's a status symbol for your type of girl. You wear your six-months' anorexia like a badge of honour. You think it gives you an edge…? It makes you a stereotype! That's why when someone talks to you about their depression you can bat it aside with that shit about… 'If only you had a girlfriend you'd be feeling a lot better.' Christ, if we let you drone on you'd be singing, 'Cheer up, Charlie'.

WILLIAM. *Willy Wonka's Chocolate Factory…* I HATE that fucking film! Get out of here, Emily!

EVA. We want people who are here for Jim.

EMILY. I'm here for Jim!

WILLIAM. Someone who understands his problem. Who gets the cause.

JIM. What cause?

EMILY. What, Jim is your cause now?!

WILLIAM. We're here one hundred per cent and on twenty-four-hour call. Jim's feeling cut up over something and we're here to listen and advise him, understood?!

EVA. That's right.

WILLIAM. We don't need any chaff! Jim doesn't need some ex-anorexic pony-rider whining little *TV Digest* sound bites!

EVA. Put simply…

WILLIAM. Piss off!

A pause. WILLIAM *and* EVA *are laughing.* EMILY *looks very upset.*

EVA. Is she gone?

WILLIAM. Hardly matters.

JACK. I thought we were supposed to be friends.

EVA. Silly cow.

JIM. Maybe she didn't mean what you think.

WILLIAM. There's no need to defend her, Jim. She's not needed.

JACK. Anorexia's terrible. You shouldn't have said those things.

EVA. Forget about her... she's debris. We're here for Jim. What about you, Jack?

JACK. Yeah, I suppose.

WILLIAM. A wonderful vote of confidence there... maybe a bit more conviction, Funny Man?

JACK. Well, no offence, Jim... but we're your age... shouldn't you be taking advice from a doctor maybe?

JIM. Well, I was actually thinking...

EVA. Christ, Jack, that's so fucking cruel. Don't you get it? He doesn't have anyone. We're it!

JACK. Look, all I'm saying...

WILLIAM. Jack!

A pause.

Can we step into Kylie's Chatroom? I want to talk to you in private.

A pause.

JACK. Okay.

Lights.

EVA *is left with* JIM *in the room.*

JIM. That was all a bit weird.

EVA. Well, you don't have to worry about that now.

JIM. Okay then.

EVA. So tell me about the day your father went missing.

JIM. Well, it's quite important… shouldn't I wait for the two boys to come back?

EVA *looks exasperated.*

EVA (*sweetly*). I'll get them my notes.

JIM. All right then.

A pause.

Right, well, I'm six years old and my three brothers are going away with my mother for the weekend… a treat for something or other. My dad's staying behind and my mother says that he's to look after me. That it would be a chance for us to bond. So they're gone and me and my dad are sat at the kitchen table looking at each other. Like we're looking at each other for the first time, you know. He asks me what I want to do and straight away I say I want to go and see the penguins in the zoo. When I was six I was going through some mad penguin obsession. I used to dress up as a penguin at dinner times and always ask for fish fingers… stuff like that. If it wasn't penguins it was cowboys. Cowboys were cool. A penguin costumed as a cowboy was always a step too far, funnily enough. (*Laughs a little.*)

EVA (*groans to herself*). Oh my God.

JIM. So we go to the zoo and I wear my cowboy outfit… get my gun and holster, my hat and all that. We get the bus and it's sort of funny to see my dad on a bus and away from the house. We start to have this chat about when I was born and what a really fat baby I was… but how after a week or so I stopped eating any food and everyone was very worried. That he was very worried. That he was so happy when I got better and they could take me home. (*Slight pause.*) We're in the zoo and I go straight to the penguins. Standing in my cowboy gear… looking at the penguins… having such a great chat to my dad on the bus… it was a perfect childhood day. (*Pause.*) He lets go of my hand and says he'll be back with my choc ice. And he goes. (*Pause.*) He's gone. (*Pause.*)

I'm happy looking at the penguins but it's an hour since he's left and I go to look for him. I'm walking about the zoo and I'm not worried yet. And I don't talk to anyone. I leave the zoo and I go to the bus stop we got off at earlier. I get on the bus. I tell the driver my address. He asks where my parents are and I say they're at home waiting for me. I stay on the bus in the seat nearest the driver. After a while we end up at the end of our street and the driver says, 'So long, cowboy.' (*Smiles a little*.) He was nice. (*Pause*.) I get the key from under the mat and open the door and go inside the house. And I'm alone there. I take off my cowboy clothes and hang up my hat and holster. It being Saturday night I have a bath and get into my pyjamas because my dad would have liked that. I have a glass of milk and some biscuits and watch *Stars in Their Eyes* 'cause that was his favourite programme on the telly. (*Slight pause*.) It's getting dark outside and I start to worry. The house is feeling too big so I get my quilt and take it into the bathroom and lock the bathroom door and it feels safer with the door locked so I stay in there. And he's not coming back. (*Pause*.) He's never coming back. (*Pause*.) I stay there for two days.

EVA *looks bored*.

WILLIAM *talks in private to* JACK.

WILLIAM. It will be a laugh. Right now, we're all he has. We're there for him 24/7… it will be a blast! Eva gets it, why can't you? He's our cause. Let's let him talk. Mess him up a bit. See how far he'll go.

JACK *says nothing*.

Are you there, Jack? Are you with the cause, Jack? (*Calls in 'a mummy voice'*.) Ohh, Jack?!

A pause.

JACK. What next?

WILLIAM *smiles*.

Lights and music.

EVA *and* WILLIAM *sit on either side of* JIM. *They each have a small notebook and take notes as we see* JIM *talking non-stop.* JACK *sits just away from them. After one-and-a-half minutes the music cuts.* EVA *and* WILLIAM *read out their notes.*

EVA. A lower-middle-class family with your mother having notions above her status. Hence the extra-curricular activities. The rugby, the horse-riding, the rowing classes…

WILLIAM. Et cetera, et cetera, et cetera.

EVA. At the age of four and you realise that the children on your street laugh at your brothers for their aggressive social climbing.

WILLIAM. And the people in the rowing club laugh at them for wearing the pikiest clothes.

EVA. Your first feelings of anxiety when you understand that you are living in a family hated by everyone and that you are one of them.

JIM. Right.

WILLIAM. You decide to stay indoors. But being the youngest brother to brothers built on the rugby field, they adopt you as their plaything and later their punchbag.

EVA. At the age of five you go back outside to play with the other children.

WILLIAM. Only to see that bonds of friendship have already been formed.

EVA. And there is little room for a small tubby toddler who has an unhealthy obsession for penguins.

WILLIAM. You are all alone but you do find a friend in… ahhh?

JIM. Timmy.

EVA (*sighs*). Little Timmy Timmons.

JIM. Yeah.

WILLIAM. A tiny six-year-old with severe bronchial problems who has to drag an oxygen canister behind him. When the other children play road-football...

EVA.... you are watching Timmy's mother slap phlegm out of Timmy's chronic lungs and into a Tesco bag.

WILLIAM. Watching this at the age of six you have your first thoughts on your own mortality.

JIM. True.

WILLIAM. One momentous day, your father leaves you in the zoo, leaving the family in the shit.

EVA. Your mother is forced into getting her very first job. She finds work in a petrol station, ending all her dreams of the posh life and throwing her into a depression eased only by...

WILLIAM.... gin and tonic... the tonic being...

EVA.... Valium.

WILLIAM. Your best friend Timmy dies, not from the tragic weakening of his lungs in the middle of the night...

EVA.... but a speeding Ford Mondeo which flattens his trailing oxygen canister and leaves Timmy walking zombie-like through the mean streets of Chiswick as the other children shout...

WILLIAM.... 'Spa-Boy!'

EVA. The day of Timmy's funeral, you take your first Valium. You are aged eight.

JIM. Eight and a half!

EVA (*correcting her notes*). Eight and a half!

WILLIAM. You try to make contact with your dad by placing leaflets on lamp posts but to no avail.

EVA. You try to make friends with anyone you meet by ingratiating yourself to whatever they want you to be...

WILLIAM. ... but to no avail. You decide to retreat back into the indoors and your Neanderthal brothers' daily beatings.

EVA. You hide yourself in books of the occult which leads to a period of bed-wetting.

JIM. Is that important?

EVA. Oh, definitely!

WILLIAM. You briefly turn to religion and take part in a Passion play where you realise that you hate Jesus Christ only slightly less than you hate your mother, the Virgin Mary.

EVA. At thirteen you read your first porn which only creates more of a distance between you and those girls you will never get to touch.

WILLIAM. You hate yourself and decide to stop communicating with other people entirely. Your life is directionless.

JIM (*almost hyperventilating*). Jesus.

EVA. The next two years are a sad cocktail of home-made beer, the odd Valium and the odd shot of whiskey.

WILLIAM. Nights begin to take on a pattern of aggressive self-analysis until one night you're talking to an American bloke on the internet who's planning to kill himself. His unfortunate name is Chad.

EVA. Like Chad and the others in the suicide club... you reach a moment of recognition. You are searching for that elusive purpose.

WILLIAM. A purpose. (*Closes his notebook.*) Right.

A pause.

JIM (*sighs*). A purpose. Fuck. Fifteen years. It's so depressing.

EVA. If it wasn't such a tragic life it would make a very funny musical.

WILLIAM. I don't think you've ever been given a chance. For some reason you're the one who always gets burnt.

JIM. But why me?

WILLIAM. You can't take responsibility for what people have done to you or what people think of you, Jim.

EVA. The reasons why people have done those things isn't something you have control over. 'Why me?' is a pointless question. Stupid even.

JIM. Right. Sorry.

WILLIAM. What you are feeling right now, this moment, that's all that matters. Concentrate on that.

JACK. But try and think more positive...

EVA. Oh, shut up, Jack!

JACK. But fuck it, guys, all this talk...

WILLIAM. Jack!!

JACK. No, this is just bullshit. You're just highlighting all the shit that's happened to Jim. Jim, listen to me. Things have been hard, I can see that...

WILLIAM. You don't care about Jim.

JIM. Yes I care!

WILLIAM. Why don't you tell him what you said to us earlier.

JACK. What are you talking about?!

WILLIAM. Be honest with him. Tell him.

EVA. Tell him, Jack!

JIM. What did you say, Jack?

EVA. I told him about your dad and how he left you when you were a child and Jack started laughing.

JACK. What?

EVA. From the outset, Jack's been saying that you sounded like a spoilt little twat who needed a kick in the arse.

JIM. You said that, Jack?

JACK. No!

WILLIAM. He can't be trusted, Jim. He's one of these hard-working lower-class types. Doesn't even live in Chiswick. He's a Brixton-boy or something. Apple of his mother's eye. He makes himself out to be everybody's friend. He's a backstabbing bastard.

JACK. Fuck off...

EVA. Nothing worse than someone ashamed of their background, is there, William? Some eager beaver affecting a voice to get on.

JACK. Oh, Jesus...

EVA. Sitting around the dinner table looking at the dumb faces and cringing at the stupid chit-chat of family life.

WILLIAM. Can't you see him! The Little Lord Fauntleroy of Stockwell stuck in his bedroom and dreaming of escape.

EVA. He thinks that way about his own family, then friends must mean shit.

WILLIAM. He's no friends. It's all virtual with Jack. Can't have people seeing him for what he really is.

EVA. What does Jim mean to the superior Jack, I wonder?

WILLIAM. Some whingeing twerp.

EVA. Some middle-class quack.

WILLIAM. A gutless jibbering child.

EVA. One of life's morons.

WILLIAM. A spoilt imbecile.

EVA. A mollycoddled spastic.

JACK. Jim, please…

JIM. Shut up, Jack!

JACK. But this is…

WILLIAM. Jack, you worthless piece of shit! Why don't you take your snobby elitist backside and just fuck off back downstairs to an evening of Pringles and Sky One!

EVA *laughs*.

EVA (*to herself*). Too good.

JACK (*snaps*). Fuck it!!

Lights down on JACK.

WILLIAM. So sorry you had to hear all that, Jim.

JIM. And he seemed like such a good person.

WILLIAM. I know… and you think you know someone.

EVA. Continue then, William.

A pause.

WILLIAM. Jim?

JIM. I'm listening.

WILLIAM. You have to focus on your anger and channel it into something that will get all those people in your past back.

JIM. How do you mean?

A pause.

WILLIAM. How do you think you would hurt your mother for all those years of neglect? All those years she treated you like nothing.

JIM. Well, I've been fighting her for so long now…

EVA. But she doesn't listen to you, does she?

JIM. No, she doesn't. And it doesn't make me feel any better.

EVA. So?

A pause.

JIM. I've been thinking about if she came into my room in the morning and if I had done something... (*Pause.*) like maybe I've cut my wrists or taken pills or something... I can imagine her face.

EVA. Bitch.

WILLIAM. She'd be crushed. The guilt would kill her.

JIM. Yeah, I suppose it would.

A pause.

But I don't know if I'm ready to do that.

WILLIAM *and* EVA *look irritated. A pause.* WILLIAM *settles himself.*

WILLIAM. Jim?

JIM. Yes.

WILLIAM. Me and Eva can't imagine what your life's been really like. It just sounds so...? so sad. Without hope, probably.

EVA *laughs a bit.*

But we've been giving up our time and listening to you for the past few nights, haven't we?

JIM. Yeah. And thanks, lads, really.

WILLIAM. I only want you to do one thing for me, all right?

JIM. Yeah, sure, William. Whatever it is.

WILLIAM. I want you to ask yourself two questions before you go to sleep tonight. Do you have a pen and paper to write the questions down?

JIM. Emmm? Yeah, go on.

WILLIAM. 'Why is it people treat me like I'm nothing?'

JIM *speaks the lines as he writes them down.*

'If no one cares about my life, why should I care?'

Finished writing them he silently reads them back.

Suddenly something's got JIM'*s attention. He looks sharply to his left.*

JIM. It's two o'clock in the morning and my mother's outside hoovering the stairs and landing. Tonight my three idiot brothers called me a freak for not wanting brown sauce on my quiche. (*Slight pause.*) I better go. Thanks, guys.

WILLIAM. Sweet dreams.

JIM *stands up and away from his seat.*

EVA. He's ours.

Music. The Prodigy's 'Smack My Bitch Up' screams along. WILLIAM *and* EVA *burst out laughing.*

The music ends abruptly.

Lights up on JACK, EMILY *and* LAURA.

LAURA. The rule in the room is we don't give advice.

JACK. He spoke about you. He spoke about this place…

LAURA. I can't help him! So if you're not here for anything else…

EMILY. But he might listen to you.

LAURA. If he's suicidal the last thing he needs is someone else giving their half-arsed opinions. It doesn't help, believe me.

JACK. It's not like that. He's being talked into doing something…

LAURA. I can't get involved! Look, what I do is sit here and listen to people my age who have these urges to hurt themselves. Most of the time they don't do anything. A lot of the time they just need to know that someone is listening to them because they either feel they don't have anyone or they actually don't have anyone. That's all I do!

JACK. But right now the only people he has are two strangers who want to see him do something to himself.

LAURA. I don't go into other rooms any more. There's too much shit that goes on. People get hurt.

EMILY. Exactly.

LAURA *stands away from her seat. She's agitated. A pause.*

JACK. Christ! Are you still there? Laura? Laura, please?!

LAURA. If you want to pass on my e-mail to him it's laura15%@aol...

JACK. Oh, for fuck's sake! You don't have to talk if you don't want to. Just come and you'll see. If it gets too much you can always get out. We'll be right there with you.

LAURA. But who are you? How do I know I can trust you?

EMILY. I started a mathematics club in school called the Brainiacs. I've never so much as looked at a boy. There's nothing I'd like more than to get out of this hideous body, to be able to forget the difference between common and natural logarithms.

JACK. Emily...?

EMILY. To be able to surprise myself. Last night I had a dream and I swear to God I think I experienced my first orgasm. Today, in looking back over the details of the dream, all I can remember is Stephen Hawking asking me to change his batteries! Believe me, Laura, you can trust me! I am a trustworthy person. What we all need to do here is take our heads out of our arses and try and do fucking something!

LAURA *remains silent.*

Are you there?!

Music and The Prodigy's 'Smack My Bitch Up' resumes from where it was cut. WILLIAM *and* EVA *place their seats to face* EMILY *and* JACK. JIM *places his seat between the two groups. Lastly* LAURA *places her seat next to* JIM*'s. The whole six stand and look at each other like they're sizing each other up for the big showdown.* JACK *is the first to sit, then* EMILY, LAURA, JIM, EVA *and finally* WILLIAM.

As WILLIAM *sits the music cuts out.*

Lights.

EVA. As little babies you can't do any wrong, can you, William? You're bloody perfect! All you do is eat, shit, laugh, cry, sleep, don't sleep, but you're loved. And I suppose you're loved because your parents have this blank page, don't they? And all their hopes can be projected onto this beautiful little blob.

WILLIAM. And the blob can't disappoint because it's just a beautiful little blob. But of course that only lasts a few months until BANG!

EVA. Suddenly the blob's a little too hungry, a little too loud, a little less beautiful.

WILLIAM. And then it's a little toddler and its character is forming and it's only right to be a bit more critical now that it's a little toddler. Too quiet, too shy, too aggressive, can't stop eating, a little too cranky...

EVA. ... blah blah blah blah blah blah...

WILLIAM. Before you know it, the toddler's ten years old and let's say that another baby is born.

EVA. Oh, typical!

WILLIAM. The ten-year-old is this big mouth to feed. This ever-growing child who disappoints, causes worry and sucks your money. Your parents' hopes are already on the next blob because at ten years of age a person is made, a character's developed.

EVA. The damage is done.

WILLIAM. It certainly was with me.

EVA. Now just imagine what the teenager means to its parents if a ten-year-old means that, Jim?

WILLIAM. Well, we're not a child, not an adult.

EVA. 'Not a Girl, Not Yet a Woman.'

WILLIAM. Oh, Eva, please!

EVA. Britney speaks the truth!

WILLIAM. A teenager is 'a sub-person'.

EVA. Not that Britney used the lyric 'sub-person'...

WILLIAM. This hormonal mess. A boy-man, a girl-woman. We're like a bad experiment.

EVA. So true.

WILLIAM. If God had really thought things through... we'd be babies born on the Monday and fully grown adults on the Tuesday, because everything else in between is this long list of fumblings, mistakes and bad skin.

EVA. Ohh, the bad skin!

WILLIAM. The teenage years.

EVA. And the voice we have, William.

WILLIAM. What voice!?

EVA. Any voice that hasn't been shaped by some shit children's writer or some draining pop star... if we do have an original thought... it's just seen as a joke, isn't it? It's a joke 'cause those adults who have lived through these years remember them with complete and utter embarrassment.

WILLIAM. It's not that we're misunderstood or not understood at all.

EVA. No.

WILLIAM. They understand us completely because they've lived through these years and see it as their right...

EVA. As their adult duty!

WILLIAM. ... to patronise us with the words, 'Whatever you're going through, you'll get through it.'

EVA. 'Now clean that bloody bedroom, bitch!'

WILLIAM. Your mother would use 'bitch'?

EVA. By fifteen you've realised that the individual doesn't mean shit and the average teenager is seen as the big embarrassing joke. We're all just folded up neatly and placed into a box marked 'The Awkward Years'. But when you allow yourself to be summed up that simply... from fifteen onwards you will live the rest of your life through these different phases. You will be summed up into little boxes until they stick you in your final box and shove you in the ground. Guaranteed. Only a few teenagers make a stand. Only a few brave souls make a statement. Teenagers like you, Jim.

JIM. Like me?

WILLIAM. I was thinking that Jim's depression allows him to see things clearer than us. He's been neglected by his family and friends so that maybe his isolation represents perfectly the average teenager's plight. It's like he's expressing important issues in a creative way. It's poetry. It's a metaphor, Eva.

EVA. It's quite brilliant, Will.

WILLIAM. But you know, Jim, maybe the more public you make it, the more of a statement you'd be making.

EVA. What an excellent idea!

JIM. How do you mean?

WILLIAM. Imagine all those forgotten teenagers you'd be speaking for if you killed yourself publicly. You'd be a hero. A legend.

EVA. Very brave. Very romantic. Sexy even.

JIM. Do it in public?

A pause.

I'm not too sure about that.

WILLIAM. Maybe show it over the internet then. Would it be easier in your bedroom?

JIM. Yeah, I suppose.

EVA. It sort of seems right that he remains alone. That people see him die like that.

WILLIAM. Well, it's stronger, isn't it?

EVA. Definitely.

A pause.

JIM. Well, I'm usually alone anyway, so... And for the past few weeks I don't like being out in public places so much. Seems easier if I do it here.

EVA. Can you get a webcam to broadcast it?

JIM. My brother Jonathan has one.

WILLIAM. Perfect.

Slight pause.

JIM. Of course, he'd kill me if he found me using it.

WILLIAM. Well, we wouldn't want that to happen, would we?

EVA. It sort of steals your thunder.

JIM. Yeah.

WILLIAM *and* EVA *laugh.*

LAURA. Jim, this is Laura.

A pause.

EVA. And who are you?

EMILY. She's come in with us.

LAURA. I've spoken with Jim before. We know each other.

WILLIAM. You're a friend of his?

LAURA. Why exactly are you harassing him like that?

WILLIAM. We're here for Jim. Do you know what state he's in?!

LAURA. I know he's not feeling well.

EVA. What!?

LAURA. He hasn't been feeling good about himself. He's lonely. He feels detached.

EVA. He's suicidal! He's ready to take his life.

JACK. Which is what you want!

WILLIAM. Oh, piss off, Jack!

LAURA. Why is it you're doing this?

WILLIAM. We're his friends.

EMILY. No you're not.

WILLIAM. We didn't abandon him like you two. He came to us looking for advice and we've been making things clear for him.

LAURA. You're talking to him like there's no options. You're making him believe that there's nothing else. That suicide is some romantic gesture. Like one fifteen-year-old's death will be held up by other fifteen-year-olds and celebrated for something. Will make a big statement for all those 'trapped' average teenagers! If you think of yourself as some blob who's moulded into this empty child and sent on a set pattern through life… if you think that… it will happen.

WILLIAM. It will happen! Choices are made and choices will be made where you have no control. Your life is set!

LAURA. That's shit! Every single moment in life there's possibilities.

WILLIAM *gets up from his seat and snaps:*

WILLIAM. Bitch!

LAURA. The statement being made is yours. But what are you saying, William? That you've got power? That you're smart enough to take advantage of someone vulnerable and talk them into the corner where they might kill themselves?! And this is some joke to you two, right?! Some big comedy. Because you can't see him, it's easier. It's easier when you don't have to see a dead boy and just imagine it like you read it in a book or something. It's easier than murder, isn't it, William, 'cause Jim's faceless to you… but it's just like murder. In these rooms, words are power and you and that bitch have all the right words…

WILLIAM. Eva, come on!

EVA (*to herself*). Ah fuck this.

She leaves.

WILLIAM. You've tried to kill yourself but chickened out, haven't you?! You think I'm going to allow Jim to be lectured by some whingeing coward like you. Some New Age happy-clappy princess! Jim has real problems.

LAURA. This isn't some competition about who's the most sad here! And if you need to know, you dick, I have tried to kill myself! I did slit my wrists. It did come from a very real place! But I'm happy I'm alive. And some days are better than others and the future scares me but I'm ready for the struggle! And I like the struggle! I like it a lot more than being dead and stuck in the ground and watching over my family and friends who I've torn apart. Stay alive and they can help me! There's always a life!

WILLIAM. You're one of those sad girls who hangs out in suicide chatrooms. Who just sits there like some black hole. All silent and dumb and soaking up the sad stories. Wallowing in other people's pain. What statement are you making, bitch!? You talk about a life of possibilities, choice, love, happiness… but I bet you'd like nothing more than a world of sad, morose fifteen-year-olds draining on about their pathetic lives. Well, why not support those who want to kill themselves? Why not allow them do it?! They're like the front line, aren't they?! The public face of our gloom, printed in the papers and shown on the telly! They need our support to do the brave thing... to do the decent thing. To get rid of the chaff and make a true revolutionary teenager! So do the decent thing, you worthless cow! Next time don't cry out to Mummy and Daddy! Just do it!

JIM (*quiet*). Stop.

A pause.

I'm fifteen and my life is mine to do with it as I please.

A pause.

Five of us are from the same area. Tomorrow at one o'clock I want you to be at the McDonald's on the high street. I want you to be there because I can't be in my bedroom any more. Maybe I'll do it quietly but I want you to see me do it.

A pause.

LAURA. Jim, I'm still here to talk to.

A pause.

JIM. You know I don't think I can listen to any more talking.

A pause.

Let's finish this.

'Dawn' from the Man with a Movie Camera *album by The Cinematic Orchestra is heard underneath all of* JIM's *final speech.*

JIM *talks to the audience.*

A large screen projects his journey down the high street and into McDonald's. The quality of the filming fairly bleached and ghostly. LAURA *places a chair with her back to the audience and watches the film.*

It's funny but I slept well. Probably the best sleep I've had in months. I left the house with my bag full of stuff and there was no one there. My mother was working her shift in the petrol station and my brothers were at this American wrestling thing that was happening in Earl's Court. I got the bus and there was this man with his young son which got me thinking about me and dad and the zoo and the cowboy outfit… and all that. Seemed appropriate that I would see them. Typical. In the bus I started to think about all those thousands of teenagers who kill themselves every year. Somebody would be killing themselves right now maybe… while a number of others would have it all planned out. And a lot of them are doing it because… they really are very ill. And some are doing it because they're alone… or maybe they're sad because someone hurt them somehow. There are so many reasons to do it. And I started thinking about all the families and friends who are left behind and the regret that must eat them up. It's all so quiet and violent. (*Pause*.) I got off the bus and walked through the streets and imagined all the ghosts of the dead teenagers looking at me. And what were they thinking? And what would they say to me? It's like they all follow me down the high street and into McDonald's. And they watch me buy some chicken nuggets and a Coke and find a table. And the angels see me taking out my camera.

The film captures WILLIAM, EVA, JACK *and* EMILY *dotted around the restaurant, just faces in the crowd.*

We get a flash of a gun on JIM*'s table. It's a toy gun but at this point it reads like it could be real.*

In this room those angels are waiting for me. And I don't see myself as anything other than me. I don't imagine what I'm about to do is making a big statement or speaking out for millions of teenagers. I'm alone.

The camera finally rests on JIM *sitting alone at his table.*

I give the camera to this ten-year-old boy to hold. I tell him to point it at me and the table.

During the following, we see JIM *take things out of his bag. A cowboy hat, a sheriff's badge and a holster. People around him start to look at him as he carefully gets into the outfit.*

There's no question but I've been very sad about things. And I'm probably like thousands of teenagers who get depressed. It's almost enough for me to know that someone is there for me and someone is listening. But I had to do something for me. I had to grow up fast when my father left and it's as simple as that. And I really miss him and I can't understand why he's gone. Something that simple can mess you up for a long time.

He has taken an iPod out of his bag with two little speakers.

When you're six and wearing a cowboy outfit and looking at penguins you shouldn't be made to grow up so fast. But I was. And I tore myself up over it for years and tried to find answers but honestly… what can a child do?

A pause.

I just want my childhood back.

JIM *exhales sharply, puts his gun in his holster and quickly stands on the table. He presses the iPod and the song 'Rawhide' is heard through the speakers.*

He closes his eyes and just stays still. People around him are smiling and laughing.

The film goes into slow motion as it moves around his still-upright body, his eyes closed, a small smile appearing on his face.

We watch him for some time until a security guard drags him down.

The screen cuts to the lyrics of 'Rawhide' as the song is pumped into the auditorium.

After the first chorus, JIM *sits down on his seat for the remainder of the song.*

A final crack of the whip and 'Rawhide' ends and the screen cuts out.

A pause as we watch JIM *and* LAURA *sitting in their seats looking at each other.*

Then:

LAURA. Everything all right now?

JIM. Yeah. (*Slight pause.*) You?

LAURA. Yeah. (*Slight pause. A little hesitant.*) Thanks for sending the film, Jim. It was good. (*Pause.*) It helped.

JIM. Good.

A pause.

Will we talk about something?

LAURA (*smiling*). What will we talk about?

A pause. JIM *thinks really hard and his mind finally settles on:*

JIM. Bunny rabbits.

They both smile.

Music. 'A Little Respect' by Wheatus is heard.

We hear the first verse as JIM *and* LAURA *talk about bunny rabbits. It's a conversation we're not allowed hear.*

From above, bubbles float down on them.

LAURA *catches one in her hand.*

As the chorus pumps in we cut to:

Blackout.

'A Little Respect' continues through the curtain call.

The End.

ENDA WALSH

Enda Walsh was born in Dublin and now lives in London. His plays include a radical adaptation of *A Christmas Carol* (Corcadorca, 1994), *The Ginger Ale Boy* (Corcadorca, 1995), *Disco Pigs* (Corcadorca, 1996, then Traverse Theatre, Edinburgh, 1997; winner of the 1997 Stewart Parker Award and the 1997 George Devine Award), *Sucking Dublin* (Abbey Theatre, Dublin, 1997), *misterman* (Corcadorca, 1999), *bedbound* (The New Theatre, Dublin, 2000, then Traverse Theatre, 2001, and Royal Court Theatre Upstairs, 2002), two short plays, *How These Men Talk* (Zürich Schauspielhaus, 2004) and *Lynndie's Gotta Gun* for Artistas Unidos (Lisbon's National Theatre, 2005), *The Small Things* (Paines Plough at the Menier Chocolate Factory, London, 2005), *Chatroom* (National Theatre, 2005), *The Walworth Farce* (Druid Theatre, Galway, 2006, then Traverse Theatre, 2007; winner of Fringe First Award, 2007), *The New Electric Ballroom* (Kammerspiele, Munich, 2005, then Druid Theatre, Galway, and Traverse Theatre, 2008; winner of Theater Heute's Best Foreign Play, 2005, Fringe First Award, 2008, Best New Play, Irish Times Theatre Awards, 2008), *Delirium*, an adaptation of Dostoevsky's *The Brothers Karamazov* (for Theatre O, Abbey Theatre and Barbican, 2008), *Penelope* (Traverse Theatre, 2010, then Hampstead Theatre, 2011; winner of Fringe First Award, 2010). *Disco Pigs* and *bedbound* have been translated into eighteen languages and have had productions throughout Europe.

His plays for radio include *Four Big Days in the Life of Dessie Banks* for RTÉ, which won the IPA Radio Drama Award, and *The Monotonous Life of Little Miss P* for the BBC, which was commended at the Grand Prix, Berlin. His 2008 biopic *Hunger* told the story of the final days of IRA hunger striker Bobby Sands and won awards including the Caméra d'Or at the Cannes Film Festival and the Heartbeat Award at the Dinard International Film Festival. It was nominated for seven BIFAs (including Best Screenplay), six British Film and Television Awards (including Best Screenplay and Best Independent Film) and BAFTA's Outstanding British Film Award 2009.